A FARM DIES
ONCE A YEAR

A FARM DIES ONCE A YEAR

A Memoir

ARLO CRAWFORD

HENRY HOLT AND COMPANY · NEW YORK

Henry Holt and Company, LLC
Publishers since 1866
175 Fifth Avenue
New York, New York 10010
www.henryholt.com

Henry Holt® and 🅜 ® are registered trademarks of
Henry Holt and Company, LLC.

Library of Congress Cataloging-in-Publication Data

Crawford, Arlo.
   A farm dies once a year : a memoir / Arlo Crawford.—First edition.
     pages cm
   ISBN 978-0-8050-9816-7 (hardback)—ISBN 978-0-8050-9817-4
(electronic book)   1. Crawford, Arlo.   2. Crawford, Arlo—Family.
3. Farmers—Pennsylvania—Biography.   4. Family farms—Pennsylvania.
5. Fathers and sons—Pennsylvania.   6. New Morning Farm (Farm)
7. Farm life—Pennsylvania.   8. Work—Philosophy.   9. Pennsylvania—
Social life and customs.   10. Career changes—Case studies.   I. Title.
   S521.5.P4C73 2014
   630.92—dc23
   [B]
                                                          2013031096

Henry Holt books are available for special promotions and premiums.
For details contact: Director, Special Markets.

First Edition 2014

Designed by Meryl Sussman Levavi

Printed in the United States of America

1   3   5   7   9   10   8   6   4   2

For my mother and father

"People believe a little too easily that the function of the sun is to help the cabbages along."

—GUSTAVE FLAUBERT

A FARM DIES
ONCE A YEAR

1

When I was thirty-one years old, I went home to spend a summer with my mother and father on the farm in Pennsylvania where I grew up. I left Massachusetts in late morning, drove the last part of the turnpike in the early dusk, and left the pavement in full dark. The sign for Anderson Hollow Road was chest deep in trumpet vine and stinging nettle. A rabbit skittered out across the dirt, frantic in the bright headlights and the rising dust. Beyond the trees that lined the road, the gentle fields rolled off toward the creek, and the insects crawled in the grass, and the deer grazed silently in the low places, and the fish swam among the water weeds. At the end, my parents' farm was asleep in the dark hollow, breathing deep breaths, everything growing and dying at once.

Every time I'd come back to the farm as an adult, during holidays or just to see my parents, I'd always just been a visitor.

I'd never had any interest in being a farmer, and I'd never wanted to live there. From a very young age I'd been eager to live in cities and around other people, so I'd left the farm when I was sixteen, first for boarding school, then college, then New York, and eventually Massachusetts. I went home for longer periods sometimes in those years, but just to stay a few months and earn enough money to move on to something else. The place had always made me a little anxious. It was so isolated and lonely, and the work there was so intense.

This time, I wasn't making a completely clean break from my life in Massachusetts; my girlfriend, Sarah, was going to join me at the farm in about a month. When I'd told her that I wanted to move to a farm hundreds of miles away and without any plan beyond the summer, she was upset, but eventually I convinced her that it was important to me. I wasn't making much progress in my job or other pursuits, and I wasn't really sure about what I was trying to achieve in general. After lots of discussion we decided that I would go to the farm first and spend a month while she settled her affairs. Then she'd join me, and we would work together for a few months, and when it got colder and the season ended, we'd go on and do something different, figure it out from there. Her willingness to go along with a plan like this is one of the reasons that I'd fallen in love with her.

I knew that no matter what else happened I could be busy at the farm. My parents grew almost one hundred different kinds of vegetables, among them corn, okra, eggplant, basil, red mustard, and black turnips. Green beans were harvested all summer long, along with corn, zucchini, and yellow squash.

Strawberries were a huge job in the spring, and then in the late summer there were rows after rows of raspberries to pick. In the fall there was spinach and kale, and after the frost, winter squash. And the biggest crop, the mainstay of the farm, was the tomatoes. I knew what I was getting myself into. I would have a full-time job, and my parents would pay me a standard wage.

I also knew that my life in Massachusetts felt less satisfying than it should have. I was getting older; the time for taking risks was getting shorter. Before it was too late I wanted to do something that felt important to me, or at least different than what I'd been doing before. When my parents had first come to Pennsylvania, my father shaggy since leaving the navy and my mother still with her New Hampshire accent, the farm they had purchased was a sad and run-down property at the end of a long dirt road in one of the more rural parts of Appalachia. Gambling so much of their future on that property was a huge adventure and a life-changing decision. They didn't know how they'd eventually pay for things like health insurance, vacations, and tuition, but they did it anyway, and it turned out to be a decent way of making a living.

*

My parents' very first attempt to start a farm had been on another piece of land, an hour south of where they lived now and outside a tiny town named Sleepy Creek. My father had moved there after dropping out of law school in 1972, and my mother had joined him soon after. They were young, and going "back to the land" seemed like it could be a meaningful way to live, and also a chance to have a huge amount of fun. Photographs from that time show them affecting moody poses in headbands and leather vests, or sitting in the tall grass with their lean red dogs, or posing nude with a huge bunch of freshly dug carrots. Growing vegetables didn't feel like a real job yet, and it didn't have to, because there was plenty of time to be irresponsible and free.

I was born in 1978, and by then my parents had moved to the land where they live today. The farm was a real business, and there was less time for fun. Crazy things still happened though. One of my earliest memories is falling out of a red Ford pickup truck at the only stoplight in McConnellsburg, Pennsylvania, when the rusty door latch suddenly gave way. My beautiful mother, her hair in a thick blond braid, her cutoff jeans showing her tan legs, slammed on the brakes and jumped out to scoop me up off the pavement. Everyone in town saw: the greaser farm boys at the Bedford Petroleum station, the waitress smoking outside the Little Duchess, the fat salesman at the Dodge dealership. A few years before, a story like this might have been something she could laugh about with friends over glasses of wine and a joint, but I suspect that my mother might have suddenly realized how much responsibility she had.

Even if it couldn't always be as freewheeling as it had been once, growing up on the farm was still a huge amount of fun. I spent my days barefoot, following my mother out to the little patch below the house to look for Indian arrowheads while she hoed a line of spinach. On hot days she pulled a big galvanized tub that we used for washing vegetables out into the

yard, filled it with cold water, and let me float there while the
dogs lapped at the water. My father would put me in the bucket
loader of the John Deere and raise me way up above the barnyard, and he would let me sit on the fender and keep him company while he plowed long rows in the bottom fields.

There were no other kids my age around, but there were
people everywhere, and all of them wanted to play with me.
A steady stream of apprentices, most of them just a few years
younger than my parents, lived there every summer. Almost
no one seriously thought that farming like this could be a
viable career, and most of them were there to spend a summer in Arcadian bliss. One of them would stop working to
show me how to identify wild spearmint by its square stems,
and another would walk with me after a storm to look for
fallen birds' nests. At night they would drink beer down by
the creek and teach me how to skip stones.

Our social life outside the farm was limited, but sometimes we would get in the pickup and drive down to Sleepy
Creek, where another couple still farmed on land near where
my parents had lived. There were bonfires, rough hayrides
pulled by a tractor with a tipsy driver, and corn cooked on
the open coals. The swimming hole behind the house would
be full of naked people lounging on the rocks and riding the
long arc of the rope swing that jutted out over deep water.
That couple had twin girls, just a year younger than me, and
as a kind of parlor trick their father would have them roll
joints from the pot that grew in the woods.

I was four years old when my sister, Janie, was born, and I
went to kindergarten the next fall. Things changed for us; I

couldn't wear my pajamas all day anymore, my mother had to go to PTA meetings with other mothers who wore tight curlers and carried huge purses, and my father bought a station wagon from a man who ran a produce distributor in Washington. The farm was a bigger business, with more sales but also more debt, and my father had to spend more time in his office and less time outside washing the new crop of pumpkins in the creek or getting the last few strawberry seedlings into the ground before the sun went down.

As the farm got bigger, my parents' expectation for the business grew. Against the odds, the farm had succeeded, and now someday it would be their legacy. There were a few more years for my sister and me when the farm was a place where we felt separate from the outside world, but eventually we finished school, I moved to New York and Janie to Pittsburgh, and both of us went on to do other things with our lives. The farm seemed distant and preserved at the end of its long dirt road, and very separate from my day-to-day life. Now that I was going back there, I didn't expect it to be the same as when I was a little kid. I still looked forward though to being back in my family's small kingdom in the hollow.

✳

Sarah and I lived in Cambridge, and I'd always loved living in that city. I loved how the Charles River was full of boats and how the bridges were all beautiful in different ways, and I loved the old oak trees, the uneven brick houses, and the graveyards with the toppled stones. I loved the names of the streets and the way the white spire of Memorial Church glowed in the evening above the green trees. I'd spent two mostly happy years there, eating in cafés filled with smart and beautiful girls, shopping at bookstores with piles of obscure remainders, walking through the snow to get coffee from a shop on Brattle Street that smelled like wet wool.

Sarah and I lived in a small apartment that was full of books, with an old chair to sit in and read by the open window, where the quiet sounds of the neighborhood could drift in. Our building was at 16 Chauncy Street, located in a leafy neighborhood west of Harvard Square, where the curbs were granite and the buildings were red brick. In the summer the street was vaulted over by the branches of the trees, and in the winter the snow made it quiet and lightly traveled. Our building had a black wrought-iron gate and a dark, cool lobby with a terrazzo floor. A sign noted that Vladimir Nabokov had lived there when *Lolita* was published. It was a small sign but I loved to point it out.

I worked in an art museum at Harvard called the Fogg, and every morning I walked across Cambridge Common, through the old gate of the Yard, and into the wide brick building full of old paintings. I wasn't an important employee, really just an administrator, but I felt cozy in my small office. I had a huge Helen Frankenthaler on my wall, and I liked that I was pretty much the only one who ever got to see it.

I also felt like I understood the basic rhythms of Harvard, and could find a safe niche for myself. I'd never been a student there—hadn't bothered to even apply with my middling grades and test scores—but my family did have some history at the college. In 1886, the *Boston Globe* had written of my great-grandfather John Colony that "Harvard has one of the most graceful oars that ever sat in a college boat" and that he was "one of the most perfect specimens of muscular development in the university." One of my uncles had later taught film there, and another uncle still hung a framed letter from the college in his dining room. It had been sent to inform him of his ban from campus housing for damaging his rooms during a party in the 1950s. I thought I understood some of the codes and protocols that were so valuable at Harvard, and I felt familiar enough not to be intimidated by the institution.

I did not match my great-grandfather's physical description, however. I dressed appropriately, in pink oxford shirts and a soft corduroy blazer, but it was mostly for show. For one thing I had been drinking too much. I had a chipped front tooth from getting hit in the face one night outside a bar, and I had a collapsed knuckle from punching a phone booth on Boylston Street afterward. I went to the doctor to complain about generalized aches, now of the age to secretly worry they were cancer. I was lazy and I ate badly. Unlike my great-grandfather, there wasn't very much about me that was graceful. I think I was just bored and dissatisfied.

Besides drinking, one of my favorite things to do in Cambridge was to ride a bike around aimlessly, stopping to read the blue oval historical markers that the city had installed in various places. The one on Putnam Avenue marked Fort #1, which protected the Patriot encampment from the British, and another marked the building that had housed Meigs's Elevated Railway, a steam-powered elevated monorail first tested in 1886. There was one that marked e. e. cummings's house and one for

T. S. Eliot's. At Ash Street and Memorial Drive one of the signs noted that the Newtowne Windmill had been erected here in 1630 but that it hadn't lasted because in 1632 it had been "dismantled for lack of wind."

One evening after dinner, a week or two before I left for the farm, Sarah and I went for a bike ride to have a look at the particular sights of Cambridge once more. We had two heavy three-speed bikes from the 1960s with wire baskets on the front handlebars, one yellow and one blue. We rode down the center of the shady, quiet streets, down Hawthorn and Sparks, and through the intersection where Bow meets Arrow. We watched the rowers hoist the long, white lines of their boats out of the black river, and spied in the windows of the old houses, watching professorial types reading in front of fireplaces or polishing the silver.

At the end of our ride we stopped by the Quaker Meeting House on Brattle Street and watched the moon rise over the Charles. As we turned around to go I noticed the gate of the house behind us had been left open. It was a minor historical site, the imposing colonial mansion—now painted bright yellow—where George Washington had assumed command of the Continental Army. There was no one around, and we walked up to the front of the house like we belonged there. There was so much history everywhere in Cambridge that none of it felt particularly well guarded.

The front yard was wide and deep and filled with banks of lilacs that were still fresh and new and smelled like the best part of late spring. Once we'd made entirely sure that there wasn't anyone watching us, we knelt down and crawled under a low arch of branches until we came to a patch of green. In a space enclosed by high bushes I lay on my back, and Sarah put her head on my chest. We relaxed in this green room and listened to the thwack of a tennis ball on the courts at the Cambridge Skating Club on Mount Auburn Street. After we'd lain there for a long while we crawled back out, stretched out the cricks in our legs, and gently closed the gate behind us.

It was hard for me to leave this kind of thing behind. In lots of ways the city represented everything that I'd always wanted—tradition, stability, and good taste—but it just didn't feel entirely like home. There was something missing, some vital part that always left me outside, always a visitor. Everyone seemed so engaged, as if they were discovering the secrets of the universe at Harvard or MIT, living in houses like where George Washington had slept, or taking the kids to swim at Walden Pond. I guess I figured that at the farm I'd be busy enough that I wouldn't need to worry all the time that I wasn't doing anything important with my life.

⚹

A few days later I decided to ride my bike out to Walden Pond to go swimming myself. I'd ended my job and had a few days on my hands before I was scheduled to leave. The feeling of finding myself with nothing to do on a Tuesday morning was a little thrilling. This didn't seem like the kind of day that I wanted to spend reading, but I threw my paperback copy of *Walden* in the basket of my bike just in case, and took some cash so that I could buy an ice cream cone at the little concession stand on the beach.

Most of the ride to Walden was rural, and it trailed through woods and fields. I passed a saltbox with red clapboards in a little opening in the woods, with its distinctive asymmetrical shape, and surprised two men standing under an elm tree outside smoking. We tipped our hats, and I rode back into the dappled shade. Sometimes the path would suddenly break out into open farmland, and I went through untended meadows and swampy, grown-up places where the path was raised and made of planks. In a few miles I was back on a winding paved road and coming into Lexington.

✸

I rode into town, where Paul Revere saw "the gilded weathercock swim in the moonlight as he passed," and then I rode on to Concord and past Orchard House, where Louisa May Alcott wrote *Little Women*, and then on to the Old Manse, where Emerson had grown up. Later I would ride by the birthplace of Sam Wilson, a meatpacker for the Continental Army who inspired the character of Uncle Sam.

I got to the pond and wandered down to the beach. The pond was deep and cold, gouged out of the granite by an ancient glacier, and a flat path wound its way around the shore, through tall pines and white birch. There was a pack of small boys on the beach, huddled up against each other for warmth, their bare chests tight and their lips the color of raw liver. They grabbed their crotches against the cold and ran screaming toward the frigid water.

An old woman in a dark bathing suit adjusted a bathing cap and slipped under the line of buoys that marked the swimming area. I didn't feel as brave as her, so I took off for a walk around the pond, following two girls in string bikinis up a path that was soft with pine needles. They ran ahead, and by the time I caught up, they had left the tops of their swim-suits on a rock and were easing themselves into the water, floating on their backs, breasts toward the sun.

I kept going, passing through a bank of high wild blueberry bushes where a group of teenagers were smoking pot, shush-ing each other in an exaggerated way when they saw me coming, and a few hundred yards farther on an older man with a gray ponytail was sitting down by the water with a blond girl in her twenties. I could hear the distinct cadence of Thoreau's words drift up to the path where I was walking, and I knew that he was trying to seduce her.

Three-quarters of the way around the pond I walked back down to the water and found a set of stone stairs that led to the water's edge. I sat there for a while, looking at the craw-fish poke around in the pebbles and the flickers of fish, and then I took my shirt off and dove into the cold water. After just a few seconds in the water I could feel my lungs seize up. It felt as if my blood had evacuated my center and rushed to the far reaches of my body. I rolled over on my stomach and did the dead man's float.

I swam out to where it got a little deep, but then I turned around and got out of the water to sit on the stone steps and dry in the sun. I heard a jingle of metal, and a Massachusetts state policeman came through the trees, in his jodhpurs and distinc-tive blue cap with the silly stub brim. He had a hand on his gun, and he strode through the trees with purpose. I ducked down so that he wouldn't see me, and after he was gone I drank one of the beers I'd brought and ate an orange.

I got out my copy of *Walden* and tried to read, but I felt drowsy. I had a sudden urge to mark the occasion, so I dipped the corner of the paperback in the water before I put it back in my bag. On my way back to the beach I went up into the woods to see the rectangle of cut-granite posts linked by heavy chains that marked the outline of where Thoreau's cabin had been. I sat under a tall pine tree and looked at the spot, flipped through a few damp pages of the paperback, and headed back.

The little boys were gone, and it was quiet. I looked out across the water, and in the distance I could see the old woman whom I'd seen swim out when I first arrived. She was way out now, a half mile from the shore in every direction, and I could just make out the slow windmill of her arms. I watched her for a while and thought about how nice it would feel to be all alone like that, isolated way out in the middle of the pond. It was a feeling that I was looking forward to in Pennsylvania, and it made me eager to get home and start packing.

*

I was doing the last few miles of the drive home, the dirt road that led into Anderson Hollow, and I passed the first of the three farms on this road that had been occupied when my parents first came, all abandoned now. The blue-white mercury-vapor yard lights were lit—they came on automatically, and the bulbs lasted for years—but the barnyards were empty.

The fields opposite the houses were choked with saplings and brambles and cedar trees. At one farm the planks of the barn had fallen away, exposing the bleached frame and an empty corncrib hunched over its broken ribs. At some point a huge tree had fallen and crashed through the fence that surrounded the barnyard there, but no one had bothered to fix it because there weren't cows anymore.

Even when I was little, the land around our farm had been steadily getting emptier and lonelier. Until I was thirteen or fourteen, there was still a general store, Isaiah Locke's, three miles away, with a glass-fronted cold case full of ham and milk, hardware in a shed out back, and an attic full of boots. My father bought his Red Wings there, and we kept a running bill that we paid once a month. It was gone now, though, along with the old men who used to sit and smoke on the bench that sat under the shelves of ammunition and nails. Their properties had been cut up and sold piece by piece, the cows gone to auction, the houses torn down, whole farms disappearing into weeds in just a few years.

The farm had always relied on local farmers and producers to provide some essential items, though there weren't very many of them left. My father had always taken orders from his customers in Washington, DC, for country hams from Rotz Meats outside of McConnellsburg before it went out of business in 2003. He still sold firewood all winter long, bought from small woodlots run by neighbors and trucked into the city. A man who lived near Orbisonia had moved back to town after getting a degree from Princeton and had become an obsessive blueberry grower. He lived in a tiny shack hard against Route 522 and sold his harvest to us. My father has always contracted with local women to bake pies and cookies for his market, and for a few years he sold thick, greasy potato chips from an Amish woman in Spring Run. And sometimes there was a small niche that no one would expect. The man who ran the Napa Auto Parts grew shitake mushrooms that he sold to my father for a good price, and when that was successful, he grew snails and sold them as escargot.

The area around Gettysburg was once one of the top apple-producing regions in the United States, and we did a large amount of business with the remaining orchards. On a typical trip in the late summer, we might pick up two pallets of peaches from an orchard in Waynesboro, go on for nectarines and plums in Mont Alto, head to Cashtown to get five pallets of apples, stop at the cider press on Molly Pitcher Highway to get two pallets of cider, and then stop in Fort Loudon on the way home for a pallet of cantaloupes. These people would usually ask after my father and send along a message, "More Staymans in two weeks," or "Talk to my brother on Twin Bridges Road for more Jonathans."

Working with producers farther afield has always been part of New Morning Farm too. When I was in elementary school my father and I would drive up to Cabot Creamery in Vermont every fall and buy pallets of cheese, which my mother cut into small blocks and sold at our markets. We'd visit McCutcheon Apple Products in Frederick, Maryland, run by the same family since 1938, and Bill McCutcheon would take me back into the production line to watch the apples ride the conveyor belts and pour me a mug of cider off the line. A man named Dale from northern Pennsylvania would come once a year and unload jugs of maple syrup from his trees and leave us maple candy that my sister and I tried to love but always found too sweet to really enjoy.

There were also all the other parts of running a farm that needed the help of local people. A man near Three Springs ran a tire business on his own farm, and he would pull himself away from the soap operas he watched all day in the back of his garage to patch a tractor tire. Sonny Flasher lived in Meadow Gap, and my father woke him up a few times every summer and had him come over in the middle of the night when the coolers stopped working. There were the brothers in Big Valley who specialized in fixing irrigation pumps and the feed mill in Shade Gap that filled sacks of chicken feed from a dusty shoot. The man who'd driven my school bus was an excavator, and he would come in the spring and dig culverts to improve the drainage in the fields. There were sawmills and hardware stores, mechanics and carpenters, all forming a huge network of people that my father had built up over forty years. Some of these became my father's friends and some of them didn't, but he had to rely on them all to help keep the farm going.

✳

My parents weren't old yet by any stretch, and their farm was actually growing, even taking over some of those other fields that used to be filled with alfalfa and cows and replacing them with kale and carrots. A farm though is always a temporary arrangement, and it only lasts as long as someone cares to make a living there. Although my parents sometimes talked to my little sister and me about the future of the farm, we had both made it clear that neither of us was interested in taking the place over. Still, it made me sad to think of other people owning that land, even though I didn't want it.

I knew somebody else would happily take it over. Most of the old livestock farms were gone because it had become almost impossible to make a living with the seventy or eighty head of cattle that those farms could support, but over the last thirty years farms that looked a lot like my parents' had sprung up here and there. Some of these were started by people who had left New Morning Farm and gone on to build operations of their own. A few of these were very close; Green Heron was just over the ridge, and Star Hollow a mile up the creek. Mourning Cloak, named after a butterfly, was farther to the north, started by a man who looked like Ichabod Crane, and to the south a woman who had been a field manager at New Morning now ran Sunnyside. There were at least thirty organic vegetable farms within a hundred miles. Only a few of these were started by people that my parents knew, but most of them were similar in size and philosophy.

In the late 1980s, some of these farmers realized that there were enough of them that they could organize a farmers' co-op together and gain advantages in marketing and distributing their vegetables. They met over a few winter evenings, sometimes in our kitchen, sometimes at other farms, and made a plan. They hired a man to be the organizer, and he was given an office in an old shed at the bottom of our yard. Our farm was centrally located, it had sufficient cooler space, and we had three trucks, so it was the logical place to handle the distribution. The farmers came every Thursday, in the late afternoon after work, and unloaded their produce so that it could be loaded on a truck and driven to Washington, DC.

My father had established relationships with natural food stores in Washington over his first early years in business, and the co-op started wholesaling there. Restaurants placed orders, and then larger grocery stores, and places like the French embassy. The farmers also used the co-op to sell to each other, to help pick up the slack when there were gaps in their own supplies. If there was a crop failure, one farm could supply a few weeks of green beans so that the supply would stay steady. Other farmers chose to specialize in crops that were more difficult to produce, getting very good at growing leeks or potatoes. The farmers also found new places to cooperate, like pooling their orders for potting soil or cardboard boxes in order to take advantage of volume discounts.

Once the co-op got going, the local Amish and Mennonites became a big part of the business. Small-scale vegetable production, small enough that it could be done with horses, is still a vital part of Amish life in Pennsylvania, and once an Amishman in Path Valley got his land certified as organic, the community—always entrepreneurial—recognized the opportunity. He and his neighbors started to provide tomatoes and eggplants, and they hired a man with a pickup truck to deliver their produce. Their large families helped with the fieldwork, and they were willing to grow anything that they thought would sell. One man started an operation growing kiwi berries, and another became a supplier of Jerusalem artichokes.

All the farmers still got together at regular meetings, now occasionally held at a restaurant with a function room, but also in barns and basements, too. My father was named the president of the co-op, and they formed a board. The Amishmen were prohibited by their church from joining the governance of a secular organization, but they participated in the meetings. All of these farmers spent large amounts of time alone, and these were also social occasions, providing a place to bitch and to commiserate. People shared news about troubles they had with certain crops, and others offered suggestions. Someone might discuss a new piece of equipment he'd bought, and another one a new Japanese beetle trap that he'd found effective. The Amishmen tended to keep to themselves when it came to being social, but they were friendly enough, and especially in the winter, when there was less to do at home, everyone was happy for the company. Putting all those farmers in a room together produced inevitable personality clashes and power struggles, and some of the original farmers left and others took their place, but over time the organization started to thrive.

The co-op is there today still at the bottom of our driveway, but in an even bigger building with two larger coolers. Amishmen still ride in the passenger seats of their hired pickups to drop off their watermelons and pattypan squash, and Green Heron still drops off flowers and Star Hollow brings peppers and basil. The produce goes to some of the same little natural foods stores that have held on since the 1970s, but it also goes to fancy restaurants where senators and lobbyists eat, and to the Whole Foods that have sprung up everywhere in the metropolitan area.

More than just filling the gaps now, the farmers get together every spring and figure out how they can support each other with certain crops, and our farm is heavily dependent on the co-op, both as a market to sell our vegetables and as a place to buy produce for our own markets. My father is still the president and he presides over the meetings of the farmers. It's a large business now, but also a community. In the office there's a plaque in honor of one of the early farmers, Sam Reist, who died at the age of thirty-nine, and there's still a couch where people sit and talk about beetle infestations, or about how they have an extra dog that they can't find anyone to take.

Now that there was a viable market in places like the co-op, and more people interested in practicing this kind of small-scale agriculture, I knew my parents wouldn't have any trouble finding a young couple to take over our property. This summer, then, was one more chance for me to experience the day-to-day life of it, while it was still our family's. I wanted to be there while my father worried constantly and my mother tried to comfort him and make the best of all the small disasters that were part of every season. And I wanted to appreciate all the ways it could make me feel happy: the way my mother called the dogs to come with her when she went to pick broccoli. How my father squeezed an ear of corn to see if it was ready, and then shucked it and ate it raw. How it felt to sit in the grass at the end of the day and watch a pickup come up from the lower fields, a cloud of dust hanging softly in the air behind it.

✳

The story of the ninety-five acres at the end of Anderson Hollow Road, or at least the part of it that my family was involved in, started in late February 1976, as my parents followed a real estate agent in my father's almost-new pickup. The roads were tight and winding, and then they would turn to dirt, and then sometimes, in a way that was slightly unsettling, just trail off into the woods. The agent was lost and she rolled down the window of her long, low Buick when they came to another dead end. "Lonely out here, huh?" My mother smiled tightly at her and nodded. The woman had asked the others in her office where the farm was, but the network of dirt roads was too confusing, and there was no easy way to explain it on a map.

My mother was feeling nervous about how bleak everything looked. She was used to a rural New England landscape of sugar maples, granite, and clapboard, and this Appalachian country seemed thin and used. The drive up from Sleepy Creek was a long, boring hour through the low hills, past the stubby corn and the bare black walnut trees that edged the empty fields. On the left and the right she could see the lines of the ridges running north and south, the sagging farmhouses in their long shadows. The kitchen windows were lit against the gloom, but she couldn't imagine what the people who lived there were doing with themselves, or how they filled their days.

The agent eventually found the property just as the light

was fading. The piece of land was at the end of a long dirt road that followed a loose line along a creek. It was in a hollow, surrounded on all sides by a high ridge. If she squinted, my mother could see a deer picking its way across the slope under the bare trees. Dirty snow clung to the wet places and the air smelled like mud. A few crows complained loudly. Way down below from where they were standing, she could see the creek running flat and cold and syrupy.

My father didn't want to seem too eager.

"About how many acres is this?"

"Near about seventy," the agent said.

Eventually they would buy a little more acreages, but my parents nodded their heads like this seemed about right. And it did seem right, even though an acre was an unfamiliar measure. It was almost impossible to imagine it spread out on that uneven ground, and how much of that land was part of the huge ridge that towered over everything. Even so, the land felt like it still does today—it filled the hollow in a satisfying way.

Below the barnyard, along the creek, were long bottom fields. They were flat and even with dark rich dirt, and they looked so fertile that it seemed that it would be a simple job to grow vegetables on them. I don't know if these fields sealed the deal or not, but I can imagine that they were hard to turn down. Other farmers, real ones, with previous experience, might have noticed how prone this land would be to flooding in the spring, and they would have noticed issues with drainage and soil quality. My father didn't know anything about these kinds of details yet, but he knew he liked how the dirt smelled when he broke it apart in his hands.

The other parts of the farm were less appealing. The house in particular still had a sense of the Depression around it, with a flimsy porch and fiberboard siding that was mildewed gray and sodden-looking. There was also a pigsty built out of rough locust posts, and an empty calf shed that smelled like ammonia. There was a clothesline strung between two listing wooden crosses at the bottom of the yard, and a rusty burn barrel sat behind the house, smoldering and making the air smell like burnt plastic. And looming over everything was the gray barn, the cracks between the warped boards glowing gold in the late sun.

When the agent turned her back to shuffle papers in the car, my father grinned at my mother and opened his eyes wider. She looked away, at the old house and the narrow fields, the brown grass and the dove-gray clouds, and wrapped her coat tightly around herself. If she had thought more about it she might have wondered about how far she was from her friends and family, from most things that felt familiar, but the distance would only occur to her much later. Anyway, my father didn't seem worried about it, and she would have felt silly to bring up her concerns about feeling lonely. There were two of them, after all. She turned her face up toward the sky and listened hard. She couldn't hear a thing, and she definitely liked that about the place.

My mother was twenty-seven and thought she was probably too young to own a farm. She was a hippie, she guessed, and she liked the idea of growing food, milking goats, and making fresh bread. She knew that she wasn't very ambitious in the traditional way. Her mother, back in Keene, New

Hampshire, would have been happiest if she got married, played bridge, and went to cocktail parties. My mother was good at bridge but she disliked both cocktails and parties. She felt uneasy in her family's big brick house, drowsy under the old elms, annoyed by the smell of gin and tonic.

Before she moved to Sleepy Creek to join my father in 1972 she'd first gone a much shorter distance, to a house in the woods in Nelson, New Hampshire, just a few miles north. It was a typical kind of place in the early seventies, a house where people lived together, made yogurt, and dropped acid on the weekends. She wasn't really into it, was just along for the ride, and she didn't like acid either. She told me that once the temperature in the house had dropped below zero, and that the thing she remembered best about all that time spent in Nelson, and liked the most, was how it took days and days for the plows to come after the huge snowfalls, and how they would be trapped way out there in the woods.

On the other hand, my father had always known that he wanted to be a farmer. He'd known since he was a little kid obsessed with growing vegetables in the backyard of his parents' house in Norwood, Massachusetts. At seven years old, when other kids collected baseball cards or read comic books, he was taking vegetables around the neighborhood in a red wagon, selling them door-to-door. He'd done other jobs since, but the plot in Sleepy Creek was his first attempt to make a living by farming. My mother took the train down from New Hampshire two years after he'd started the business. It was a long-distance blind date, arranged by a girlfriend of my mother's from college and a friend of my father's from the navy. It was a big risk for my mother to take that twelve-hour train ride, but my father must have seemed intriguing enough to take a chance on. Two years later they were married.

When my mother first met my father at the train station in Martinsburg, he looked like a cowboy. He was lean and tan, wore jeans, and kept his money in a worn leather billfold with a buffalo nickel on the clasp. He had long hair and a little bit of a swagger. He picked her up in a flatbed truck with the back full of tools and pushed the knives and baling wire off the seat to give her a place to sit. Then, before they went to see his fields, he stopped at Dunkin' Donuts to use a coupon he had. She didn't really mind, but she'd been on the train for a long time and didn't want a dozen donuts. It didn't matter, though. The first time my mother saw my father at the station she thought she might marry him.

My father had already been in Sleepy Creek for a few years, but he didn't feel comfortable calling himself a farmer yet, because he felt he hadn't earned it. He'd gotten through his very first season the year before—when growing vegetables was fun but still not something that he could honestly imagine making his living at—through trial and error. He was barely getting by, but he could feed himself, and he figured he could still go back to law school if things didn't work out. Then he broke his leg at the end of that summer and spent his winter of convalescence reading books and manuals about improving soil fertility and raising chickens for profit. He met three other young people who were also growing vegetables nearby. One of them had been raised on a farm and another was a lapsed Amish, and they all got to be friends. By the time my mother showed up he had learned a lot, but he knew he still had a long way to go, and the idea that someday these fields could be productive enough to generate a real income was just starting to shimmer into view.

It was on that first piece of rented land that he'd come up with a name for his new farm. It was the end of his first season and there was a party with a bonfire and bota bags of wine and the pot that his friends had been growing in the woods. He'd sat up late talking, tipsy and silly, after other people had wandered off or passed out in the grass. The conversation turned to Bob Dylan and the album he'd just released called *New Morning*. By now, in the early seventies, Dylan seemed dangerous and unpredictable. My father liked that. He murmured the first line of the song: "Can't you hear that rooster crowing." Then, partly as a joke, and with the understanding that he could always change it later, he decided to call his new business New Morning Farm.

Four years after that bonfire, he and my mother got a loan from the bank and made an offer on the property in Anderson Hollow: fifty-two thousand dollars for the seventy-five acres. Farmland was so devalued that the banker was willing to look past the fact that my parents were about to buy seventy-five acres and they didn't know what to do with it. It must have been nice to see two hopeful young people come in talking about the future, instead of another pale farmer looking for an extension on money he was pouring through a sieve. Farming had always been a hard way to make a living, but a bushel of corn just wasn't worth as much as it once had been.

The economy was already leaving traditional family farms behind, just like small manufacturers and mom and pop grocery stores.

When my parents showed up to take possession of the property that early spring, the family who'd been living in the house was still there. The man and his wife were butchering a deer in the kitchen while their little girl sat at the kitchen table with a fresh tracheotomy. The parents explained that she'd had some medical problem but didn't go into the details. The girl breathed through the hole in her neck and looked at them with solemn eyes as her parents cut up the cold deer parts with a hacksaw.

My father asked them where they were moving.

"Tammy wants to go on up to McConnellsburg but I said, hell, ain't nobody hiring, so why bother. Probably go to my pap's place in Waterfall. Yinz are welcome to stop in if yinz got any questions."

They didn't seem unhappy to be leaving; they'd lived here for a few years and now they'd be living somewhere else. Their willingness to move on without any apparent bitterness was comforting, but my mother snuck a peek inside the cardboard boxes they were stacking neatly in the bed of the pickup, and she felt a stab of guilt. The boxes, for reasons she never understood but was too nervous to ask about, were full of empty tin cans and old newspapers.

The first night my parents spent in the farmhouse might have made it clear to them just how far out in the country they really were, and how hard a project this might be. It was a cold night, and the empty rooms were raw and plain. The plaster walls were crumbling, exposing the wooden lathe. The windows rattled in their frames, and the drafts made the iron latch on the bedroom door clink faintly. The toilet and sink were down in the cellar, installed on a concrete slab under a bare lightbulb. As my mother brushed her teeth she put her hand on the wall and felt the damp seeping through the stone.

They woke up the next morning on a mattress in the middle of a bare linoleum floor, to the sound of someone beating the pin out of a metal wagon hitch in the barnyard. My mother lay in bed and watched the flies crawl on the windowpanes, and she looked around at the things they'd brought to make a home. She had a sewing machine, an ashtray set with semiprecious stones, a copy of the novel *Sometimes a Great Notion*, and a Siamese cat named Eggroll. Her red Volvo was parked outside, a gift from her stepfather before she left for her senior year of college.

My father's possessions were slightly more useful. He had a Farmall Model C tractor that he'd purchased from an old man in West Virginia for five hundred dollars, empty boxes and crates for packing vegetables, and a golden retriever–Irish setter mix named Molly Cornflake. There was a silk rug that he'd bought when he was stationed in Vietnam and a bed that he'd built out of scrap lumber. He had a wooden picnic table that he'd been using at Sleepy Creek to eat on. He also had the almost-new Ford F-150 in hunter green. He'd traded for the truck three years before, giving up the brand-new BMW that he'd paid for with his discharge money from the navy.

They went to an auction in Greencastle to find the equipment they would need to make the farm a going concern.

They walked down the rows of unfamiliar implements, looking at plows and harrows and discs. Even if a lot of the
devices looked obscure and complicated, my father knew
that he needed a plow and a few other basic things. They also
bought a kitchen table, enameled metal in a black-and-white
pattern. They bargained hard for it, staring down the pinched-
face woman who was selling it.

After a few days of getting settled my parents set about
teaching themselves to grow vegetables for a living. It was
exciting, but at the same time they were anxious, subject to a
growing panic that spring was coming and that things were
happening too fast. In the last days of winter, as the ground
thawed and the house started to smell like mildew, they sat at
the kitchen table and looked at seed catalogues and mostly
picked the things that they liked to eat: tomatoes, dill, and
Swiss chard.

The one crop that they really agonized over was the
tomatoes. It had always been my father's favorite vegetable,
and it had been the centerpiece of all the gardens he'd ever
grown. They were important to him when he was seven years
old, pulling his wagon around his neighborhood in Norwood,
and even more important when he was living in Sleepy Creek,
when he took his first crop back to Washington to sell to his
friends from law school. There was something obvious about
tomatoes, a basic legitimacy that chard or asparagus would
never have. Everybody loved the idea of buying a red tomato
that was fresh off the vine, still warm from the sun and smelling of soil, picked just hours before in the countryside beyond
the beltway. They would be easy money.

My parents also knew that marketing was part of the deal. They knew from their time at Sleepy Creek that customers in Washington would buy tomatoes from the handsome young farmer and his pretty blond wife. My father would flirt with the young women, and my mother would listen to the men while they told her how they'd always thought about moving out to the country, leaving their office jobs behind and seeing if they could make a go of it by working with their own two hands. My parents knew that they should look a little lean and hungry, but that was taken care of because they really were, and it would seem less and less like an act the longer the first summer at New Morning went on.

Once they'd chosen the varieties they wanted to plant, they spent a day building shelves in the living room and then filled them with rows of flats. They hung grow lights from the ceiling, the bulbs making the room glow a weird purple. When they were done they went to bed. All of a sudden my father was up; he had to check the old meat thermometer that he'd stuck in the flats to track the proper temperature for germination and make sure that the scrabbling sound they heard in the wall wasn't mice eating tomato seeds. My mother lay in the warm pool of the sheets and smelled the scent of wet soil sighing up through the heating vents and watched the fat drops of condensation drip down the windows.

A few days later a huge crash woke them up in the middle of the night. They rushed downstairs and found that my mother's cat had somehow upset the shelves and spilled all the flats on the living room floor. The pile of dirt and spilled seeds, with the tiniest of green shoots just bursting through, was bathed in the purple light, and everything looked ruined and ugly. My father chased the cat out the door and into the dark. Once he was done being angry they got the shelves set back up, and in the morning they replanted the seedlings. From then on they locked the cat in the basement at night and ignored the sad meows that drifted up through the heating ducts.

A few weeks later, once the seedlings were big enough, they set them out in the field. They started in the Lower Bottom, the field downstream from the Upper Bottom. They'd also planted Swiss chard and lettuce there, a small patch of spinach, and a row of dill. The field of vegetables needed constant attention, and every morning they went down and made themselves busy however they could, tending to them and coaxing them along. They filled buckets from the creek to water the rows, and they used their hands to pick at the weeds. There were so few plants that when one died it left an obvious gap in the straight green line of them.

In the first few days the tomatoes took off. They'd fertilized them with chicken manure, and it made the foliage heavy and green. The plants were growing too fast to support themselves, and when the leaves lay on the ground they developed a yellowish tinge, so they staked up each plant, tying it to an ash pole. The plants seemed healthier but still a little sickly. There were other problems too: a groundhog had been eating the peas, and there were heart-shaped deer tracks all around the crushed dill, but the tomatoes got the most attention. If they kept going like this they'd be bearing fruit in early August.

The first Saturday in June they got up at four o'clock in the morning and piled their boxes of lettuce and spinach in the metal bed of the pickup. The sun was rising as they approached Washington. They'd negotiated the use of a parking lot on a stretch of Columbia Road in Adams Morgan, and even if they had to rouse a drunk and sweep up broken glass, the lot was centrally located and busy. A few professional types, new to the gentrifying neighborhood, came out to buy things. The people who'd always lived there—bus drivers, bank tellers, and the people who worked at the McDonald's across the street—also came. My parents made a few hundred dollars, and the bills made a solid lump in my father's pocket. They went out that night to celebrate.

Back on the farm the following Monday, my father was more worried about the foliage of the tomatoes and the yellow color, almost like a spreading rash, that had developed where the plants had first lain on the ground. He looked in manuals and books and tried a few of his own ideas. In the next few weeks he sent soil off to the laboratory at the university extension, and it came back that it was deficient in lime. They borrowed a lime spreader from a neighbor and got halfway through the job before it broke. My mother crawled under the equipment and spent the next three hours with a wrench fixing the problem. Then they dragged the equipment a few more feet, and it broke again.

That night she skipped dinner and went upstairs to read. She smoked a joint, rolled out of the bag of mostly seeds and stems that she had left over from her last trip back to Sleepy Creek, and watched the pattern of the setting sun as it

played across the cracked plaster ceiling. She thought about
New Hampshire and her brothers and sisters, and how her
mother would be making a gin and tonic now in the library
of the old house on Court Street. She almost wished she
was back with her family, sitting down to the luxury of a
dinner that was made by someone else. This was an adventure though, and she could stick it out for a few more months
at least.

At night, when my mother kept busy sewing curtains or
reading, my father sat at the kitchen table and worried.
When he was outside he walked fast even though he didn't
have anywhere to go. In the early evenings he took his Win-
chester .243 and sat for hours on a rise above the fields, watching for the groundhog that was eating the dill to come out of
its burrow. He watched and watched, and then, just for something to do, he shot at one of the crows. He missed, and the
flock rose and circled above him, screaming at him, scolding.

By late July there were tomatoes on the plants. My father
walked down the rows and inspected every one of them, while
my mother pushed a wheel hoe down the line of dill. It was
hot now, uncomfortably so, and she would take breaks to sit
in the shade under the big trees that grew along the creek.
Sometimes she would go down to the water and slip out of
her clothes and lie in the current, looking up at the narrow
line of blue sky above her. Over the murmur of the water she
could hear the soft sounds of my father working, scuffling
dirt, and the dull clink of metal and the rumble of the pickup.
She ran her hands over her skin and could feel how thin she
was getting.

By mid-August it was clear that all the tomatoes were going to fail. The problem had started when the leaves at the bottom of the plants had gotten wet and started to rot. Eventually long dark cankers showed up on the stems of the plants and made them droop from the stakes they were tied to. The fruit was still there and some of it was even turning red, but they had developed the cankers too. They were suppurating black sores, little cancers. Now my father went down the row and looked at every fruit again, trying to find one, just one, that wasn't ruined, but they were all infected.

They felt that the farm was already a failure. A neighbor my mother met at the store mentioned the early blight that came around every few years. My mother went home, walked upstairs, and locked herself in the bedroom. She smoked the last of her pot, and when my father finally came to bed they didn't talk. When she woke up in the morning he was gone. He came back later that day with boxes and boxes of muddy turnips that he'd bought from a neighbor. For three days they sat outside with a metal tub and scrubbed them clean, and when they took them to market in Washington they sold every last one.

The season went on like this. Some things died, were eaten by deer, or just never produced any fruit at all. Some things thrived and produced way too much, so much that they couldn't keep up and had to leave them in the field. They looked in the classified ads and found other local people who were selling their extra beans or potatoes, and they took those to market along with their own stuff. My mother baked some bread, and they sold that beside the few boxes of green beans and the bunches of dill. Every week they set everything out on the folding tables and stacks of crates in Adams Morgan and waited for the customers to buy it all. At the end of the day they went home, counted the money, and went to bed.

By Thanksgiving the season was done. By now they were buying bins of unsorted apples from the orchards around the town of Chambersburg, picking through them, and selling the good ones. The house had a real bathroom now, and they'd set up a couch in the living room. My mother's Volvo was parked out by the unused pigsty, but it was broken down, and the weeds were already growing up around it. The walls of the house were still crumbling, but in the evenings, when the kitchen was full of the smell of cooking and Neil Young was singing on the record player, it felt cozy and warm.

One season was behind them, and they were happy. If there was another one, if they got through the long winter, they'd know more about what they were doing: no more fresh chicken shit on the tomatoes, less Swiss chard, and more dill. My father had already started talking about doing some building. He wanted to get a foundation dug for a tractor shed before the ground froze. They hadn't accomplished everything that they'd set out to do, but the most important bills were paid, they had a roof over their head, and they had a plan, which seemed about all they could ask for.

✳

I was on the very last part of my drive home from Massachusetts, the last quarter mile where the road ran straight for a short stretch before it went around a wide curve and down the hill into the deepest part of the hollow. I stopped the car and rolled down the window to let the cool night air in. The rows of vegetables stretched across the rise beside the road, black on black under the faint moon, and the early-summer air smelled like dust and chlorophyll. I shut off the ignition and sat in the dark. Behind everything I could see the huge black shape of the ridge. Parked in the field, silhouetted against the starry sky, was the Farmall Model C that my father had bought so long ago.

If I'd been asked that night if I was coming home because I was proud of my parents, of how they'd established themselves, it wouldn't have occurred to me to think of it that way. But a few weeks later I ran a package to the post office and the woman behind the counter saw the return address. She said, "You Jim Crawford's son? How're things down there anyhow? Yinz getting plenty of beans in all this heat?" I nodded and told her that the farm was fine, that my parents were doing well. It would be the first time in a long, long time that a stranger recognized me as my father's son. It was a good feeling, and I wondered why I hadn't missed it more.

At the bottom of the road I could see one window glowing. My father's head was silhouetted there as he ate his dinner. Around him, in a wide semicircle so that he could reach everything, would be vegetables: a sliced tomato and a bowl of cold beans, a half-eaten cucumber and a bunch of radishes, and a saltshaker. There would be snap peas and asparagus. There would be slices of bread and ham, and a cold beer. Across the table my mother would be working on the crossword, concentrating hard over her pencil and drinking a glass of cold milk. They'd be sitting at the same enameled-top kitchen table.

I drove past our mailbox, which said New Morning Farm, and parked the car behind the house so my parents wouldn't see me right away. After a minute or two, one of the dogs looked around the corner of the house, saw me sitting there, and started to bark. My mother's voice came through the open kitchen window, "Hush!" I went to the front door and turned the knob. As I stepped into the bright kitchen, my mother and father both turned to me and smiled at once. I hugged them and went to pour myself a glass of water from the metal tap. It had a particular taste from the well, cold and mineral, the way water tasted when I was a little kid.

2

The next morning I lay in bed for a few minutes and listened to the rain drip from the leaves. Before I'd gone to sleep I'd seen flashes of lightning, but I'd left all the windows open anyway, and in the middle of the night a storm had started, and the wind had gusted in. Now I stretched out on the clean sheets, enjoyed the cool starchiness, and tried not to worry that I'd done the wrong thing by coming home. I felt homesick for Sarah and for Cambridge, and I wasn't sure how to get my day started. When I couldn't put it off anymore, I went downstairs. The kitchen smelled like coffee, but both my parents were already outside, and the room was empty.

In my planning before I left, I may have underestimated how difficult it would be to feel comfortable on the farm right away. It was the end of May, so the season was already in full swing. Everyone was busy, and there wouldn't be much time for anyone to welcome me home. I stood at the sink and looked out the window, down the slope toward the bottom fields. Mist rose out of the tall grass, and the trees were already steaming in the heat. The sound of a tractor drifted into the kitchen from somewhere, and I could hear someone working with a shovel, the heavy blade being kicked into the dirt and then the loose slide of stones and dirt pouring off the metal.

Part of the problem was that everyone had established a routine except for me. If I were still back in Cambridge I'd be going downstairs to get the paper from the lobby of our apartment building, eating a bowl of cereal and a banana, maybe worrying about some e-mail I'd forgot to return or an assignment I'd been putting off. At the very least I'd know what the proper steps were to get my day going: put on pants, ride bike to office, type username and password.

Standing at the sink I could see that there was something in the view that was irregular—one of the huge old trees down by the creek had fallen over in the storm the night before. Those trees were nearly a hundred years old, big oaks with spreading limbs, and I could see the tall white splinter of the broken trunk shining in the dame's rocket that grew thick along the bank. I was still staring out the window when I heard my mother's feet on the cellar stairs. The iron latch rattled and she pushed the door open, coming out into the kitchen with her hands full of oregano she'd just picked from the patch below the house.

"What's wrong?" she said.

"I hate not feeling busy."

She nodded. "Well, I've been busy all morning. Got the eggs packed and the cheese done. I should go weigh beans."

"You want to sit down with me and have a cup of coffee?"

"Let me sweep this floor first and feed the dogs."

She got the broom from where it hung behind the cellar door and swept the blue and white linoleum. The kitchen was full of things from the farm: two hand hoes hung on the wainscoting, a shovel against the door frame, an apple box full of clean laundry, strawberry boxes of clothespins, and an egg carton full of pennies. There was a pile of green beans on the counter and four rotten turnips by the sink. Beside the door was a peach basket full of cabbages. My mother moved around the kitchen, cleaning up the breakfast dishes, and then she finally sat down with me.

We sat at the table and drank cups of coffee, and she consulted one of the various lists that she wrote down all day on scraps of whatever was at hand. She wrote the bulk of her lists when she realized that she'd forgotten to do something. I came across these lists everywhere when I was at home, on paper bags, envelopes, and in the margins of books she was reading. The blank space on the back of her crossword puzzles always said something like, "Get ear medicine for barn cats." Now she scratched a job off the top of her current list and added two more to the bottom.

"So, what are you going to do today?"

"I guess I'll have some breakfast and then try and figure it out," I said.

My father's voice came over the radio that she carried with her as she moved around the farm: "Moie, Moie."

My mother's name is Emeline, the same name as my grand-mother's, but in the way of big families it had been shortened to a nickname when she was young, first to Moline, and then eventually to Moie, which rhymes with Joey.

She picked the radio up. "Yeah, go ahead, Jim."

"Do you have any idea about those beans?"

"I'm having a cup of coffee, but I'm about to go out there. Can it wait a minute?"

He didn't answer, so she sighed, pulled on her boots, and went out the front door. The dogs, all five of them, were wait-ing for her, and they barked and wagged their tails while she poured the food into their dishes. I listened to her go, heard her feet crunching in the gravel of the barnyard and my father asking her more questions over the radio she carried in her hand. I decided that I'd finish my coffee, organize my things, and then, once I felt up to it, I'd go out to the barnyard and see if I could find something to do.

The least I could do was to go down to the chicken house and get an egg to cook for breakfast. Like a lot of the jobs at the farm, this wasn't always the charming, pastoral task that most people imagined; the building itself was horrible, always smelly and dusty and filled with hot air that was almost impos-sible to breathe, and the chickens themselves were nasty and mean. Two of the dogs followed me halfway down the yard, but once they realized where I was going they stopped because they were generally scared of the chickens.

My mother had always dreamed of having a few horses,

and there had been an ill-conceived experiment with keeping a few goats years before, but a small flock of chickens was the only livestock on the farm now. The animal husbandry involved wasn't very complicated, and my father kept a small note tacked up above his desk that laid out the five variables to make a profit from the flock: price of feed, cost of labor, price of a dozen eggs, depreciation on the chicken house, and the cost of the chickens themselves. The chicken house had been built in the early 1990s, and a few times a year we shoveled out the accumulated manure and spread it somewhere on the farm that needed the fertilizer. The chickens laid eggs profitably for only a year, so in the winter my mother would place a classified ad in the paper, and local people would come and buy them two or three at a time, either for the few eggs they still produced or to butcher and eat. In the spring we got a new flock, and the cycle started over.

The two hundred birds lived in a red building at the bottom of the garden, with a line of dirty windows along one side and two doors at each end, one for people and a smaller one for the chickens. As I came closer I could see them filing out one of their little doors, down the gangplank that led to the open yard. They were mostly orderly as they descended, forming a line like commuters queuing up, but then one of them got impatient and pushed the chicken in front of her off the ramp and onto the ground. She landed in a swirl of dust and beating wings, gathered herself up, and motored off to mingle under a copse of trees.

I paused at the door of the coop, and the heavy smell of ammonia filtered through the torn screen. The day was already hot; the metal roof ticked in the sharp sun. A high, keening moan came from inside. The rusty spring on the door made a tight, strangled sound, and when the chickens heard it they all stopped and looked at me, frozen as though they had been caught doing something wrong. One chicken broke the silence with a long, loud squawk, all the others joined in, and then they went back to what they'd been doing.

The chickens slowly pooled around my feet, expecting that I was there to feed them. The feed bin was entirely infested with mice, and sometimes one of them, suddenly exposed in the light, would make a mad dash and leap onto the person lifting the lid, fall to the floor, and be devoured by the chickens, who tore it to pieces and ate it alive. I scooped up some grain and poured it on the floor, and the chickens swarmed all over it, pecking at each other.

I went to the nests to find an egg while they were distracted by the food. These were a series of metal boxes along one wall, stacked four high and filled with soft wood shavings, fronted by a wooden walkway so that a chicken could walk up and down and select the one that seemed most comfortable. Only one chicken was in the nests now, and she eyed me closely while I looked through the ones that were unoccupied. All the eggs were gone; someone had come to collect them shortly before, so I knew that I'd need to check under that single chicken, even though I didn't want to. She cocked her head, looked at me, and then looked away.

I waited until it seemed like she was calm and then plunged both hands in all at once, wrapping her wings in a tight squeeze. She tried to beat and squirm away but I held on and set her on the floor as far away from my feet as possible. She scurried off, protesting loudly, and joined the others at the pile of grain. I plucked out three eggs, still warm, and put them in the pocket of my shirt. One fell out as I was bending over, and it smashed on the floor. The chickens saw this, and there was a moment of pandemonium as they surged forward. Within seconds the spot was dry; chickens love to eat nothing more in the entire world than a broken egg.

I walked toward the door, eager to get back out into the fresh air, but the chickens refused to move, so I had to wade through them like they were a layer of deep snow. They pecked at my legs and shoes, looking for something delicious, and I shoved them back as gently as I could. Finally one took a tiny bite of the skin at my bare ankle with her sharp beak, and I kicked her away. It was gentle but she wasn't expecting it, and she flapped her wings and flew a few feet like a little broken-down biplane while the others jeered from the corners. She found a spot to stand and stared at me with her beady eyes.

✳

I stood outside in the bright sun and beat the dust out of my shirt, took deep breaths of the clean air, and inspected my ankle for blood. I cooked the eggs I'd gathered and ate them with salt and pepper, the yolks deep yellow from the bugs and grass that the chickens ate in the yard. I flipped through a seed catalogue, read a story in the local paper about a DUI and then one about a bear sighting, and had another cup of coffee. Finally I decided that I couldn't wait anymore to get busy, and I got up and went outside.

The barnyard was an open area, bound by the house, barn, tractor shed, and a packing shed. The building materials were pine, concrete blocks, tar paper, tin, and glass. Most of the buildings were painted red, the concrete blocks were white, and the barn was sided with wide gray planks. The space had formed naturally, beginning with a path worn in the dirt from the house to the barn, and the new buildings they built over the years had been fitted in the spaces between the old ones. The shape it eventually took on was organic and efficient, like a wasp's nest or a bird's bones, and even though I'd been walking around it my whole life I didn't really feel comfortable just wandering around now, especially because everyone except for me was busy working.

I walked by a pair of legs sticking out from under a manure spreader in the barnyard. The person underneath called out to me.

"Hey, can you get me the channel locks?"

"Sure. Are they in the shop?"

"Never mind," he said. "Who are you?"

I bent over and looked under the spreader.

"It's Arlo," I said.

"Arlo! I've heard about you! Welcome home!"

I reached under the equipment and we shook hands. He told me his name and that he'd been there for two months; he was friendly but the conversation was short. It was strange to come home to a busy workplace filled with people who didn't know who I was. Now that I was older, it didn't feel comfortable to think of the farm as a place for vacation, and I didn't want to look like an idle tourist. I went and got the channel locks from the workshop and handed them down to him. He used the heavy end of the wrench to beat on some corroded part and swore when the flakes of rust fell onto his face and into his mouth. I left him there and walked up to the packing shed.

The shed was a long, narrow building, with a table for washing vegetables, two coolers for storing them, areas for stacking empty boxes, and three small loading docks. I pulled open the heavy metal door of one of the coolers and stepped into the cold. It was always surprising to see the room full of vegetables—how many of them there were, stacked everywhere on pallets and on the concrete floor. There were thirty flats of strawberries against the wall, one pallet of lettuce and another one of beets, and ten boxes of cilantro that made the room smell like soap. I poked around and ate some of the strawberries, and they were cold and delicious. I took a box with me.

The three local middle-aged women who did the packing were washing lettuce, and we said hello and exchanged news. There had been a rotating cast of these women at the farm for my entire life, some working for as long as a decade, others just for a few months. New Morning wasn't their only priority—they went home to their own farms at the end of the day—and so they always stood slightly apart from the people who lived on the property. They were vital to the running of the farm, but they punched a clock and left at 5:00. The apprentices worked until the day was done, no matter the time, and so their relationship to the place was more consuming.

I headed to the basement of the barn to find some new kittens my mother had mentioned. I sat on the cool concrete floor, mewed at them, and tried to coax them close enough so I could pick one up, but when I got too close they retreated into a pile of broken window frames and stared out at me, their eyes glowing in the dark, their tiny tails twitching. I got down on my knees and held out my hand to the pile, rubbing my fingers together quickly in a way that I thought might be appealing. The kittens continued their work of purposeful climbing and scurrying.

When I came back outside the apprentices were gathered in the barnyard smoking cigarettes and picking burrs and ticks from the dogs, discussing what had to be done that day. When they saw me they stopped talking all at once. I stood in front of them blinking in the bright sun because my eyes hadn't adjusted to the glare after leaving the dark of the basement.

"Hey. I'm Arlo."

The person who'd been leading the conversation stopped and smiled at me.

"I heard you were coming home," she said. "How are you?"

"I'm great," I said, "really glad to be home. How are you?"

"Good, good. Really busy obviously, but everything is good."

There was a long pause.

"Were you playing with the kittens?"

Everyone was looking at me, waiting for my answer, and I felt stupid.

"Yeah."

I felt an impulse to somehow indicate that this was my house and that I knew the people in charge.

"Have you guys seen my dad?"

"I think he's down at the greenhouse." The apprentice in charge asked the group, "Has anyone seen Jim? Hold on, Arlo, let me call him on the radio."

She took her walkie-talkie off her belt. "Jim, Jim."

The scratchy answer came back, "Yeah, go ahead."

"Arlo is up here looking for you."

"What does he want?"

She looked at me, but I didn't have anything in particular to say.

"Never mind, don't worry about it," I said.

"Jim, he says never mind."

"OK. Hey, let me ask you, have all the lettuces down here been watered this morning? I'm looking at the Nancy you planted yesterday and it looks dry. And when is this next generation of Marathon going to get transplanted? It really needs to get done today or it's going to be too old."

She started to answer, looked at me to see if I had anything else to add, and went on talking when I shook my head. I walked back across the yard and went into the house.

There were nine apprentices this year, a group of men and women in their twenties, and they did most of the cultivating, irrigating, and harvesting on the farm. There were a few local people who worked there—the women who worked in the packing shed and a crew of teenagers who showed up sporadically to pick green beans for thirty-five cents a pound—

but, along with my mother and father, the crew of apprentices did the bulk of the work. They were dedicated to agriculture, and they took their work seriously; they rarely had time to think about much else other than what was happening with the crops.

The typical apprentice had graduated from college and was interested in food and sustainable agriculture, but hadn't come from a farming background. There was a type, people who shopped at co-ops and liked to cook with whole grains, had a few tattoos and whose politics leaned libertarian, slightly more earnest than their peers and more physically fit, but otherwise pretty normal. The only thing that really set them apart and made them special was their willingness to work every day, from early morning until dark, on a vegetable farm in the middle of nowhere.

There was a simple organization among them, sometimes more hierarchical and other times more flat, depending on the personalities involved. One person was the crew leader, and he or she was in charge of leading the morning meeting and delegating the tasks, checking in during the day to see how they were progressing, and assigning new priorities. Another person was the field manager, and this person often worked alone, generally spending a huge amount of time on a tractor. They were responsible for maintaining the fields, preparing them for planting, and then, in the winter, planting the rye grass and other cover crops that would limit erosion and renew the nutrients.

The field manager also ordered and maintained the seeds. In the winter he or she sat with my father and talked about the yields and the failures from the season before, trying to figure out what might be needed in the season to come. Certain varieties had proven themselves; we always grew Jade green beans and Marathon broccoli, for example, but the seed companies also offered new and novel varieties that needed to be tried and evaluated. My parents bought their seeds from different companies, depending on the prices and availability, but they'd always done business with a company in Maine called Johnny's Selected Seeds. That company had been started around the same time as New Morning, and our farm sometimes appeared as a photograph in the calendar they distributed to their customers in January.

The crew leader and the field manager positions were generally held by people who had been at the farm for at least three or four years, understood the larger picture of the season, and worked well with my father, since they were his main point of contact for what happened day to day, but all the apprentices had areas of serious responsibility. Someone was in charge of pest control and knew how to scout for damage in a patch of green beans, how to diagnose the severity of an infestation of beetles, and where to deploy the special wasps that served as predators for the harmful larvae. Someone else was in charge of mowing, a constant job that kept the roads clear and maintained the areas around buildings and the fields. Someone was in charge of the chickens, and another person handled the steady rhythm of the greenhouse plantings and the constant water they required. There was also a "fun committee" charged with organizing game nights and small excursions to the lake at Cowans Gap or to the carnival in Three Springs.

Each apprentice also had his or her own crops. There was a squash manager, a strawberry manager, and a corn manager. The manager was responsible for knowing how much of each vegetable was coming out of the field that day, how much would come the next week, and how much the following month. The managers watched for diseases and pest damage and reported them to the pest manager. They checked to see how much water their crop was getting and worked with the irrigation manager. They understood the ideal size and harvest date, and how to pack those vegetables in the proper way. Zucchini was always packed in a half-bushel box, the squash in neat rows across the short side of the box, and green beans always went in a bushel basket with a clean piece of white paper on top and another on the bottom. They knew where these crops were stacked in the cooler and how long each box had been there.

Some people embraced the details of these tasks, took careful notes every day, and spent hours reading research from agricultural magazines and journals about all the ways these crops could fail or thrive. Other people were less methodical, choosing to wander through their crop and understand it as a constantly evolving challenge and hoping to nudge it in the right direction. Some people developed a fierce devotion to a particular vegetable, and others hated the hand they were dealt when the crops were divvied up in the first meetings of the spring. Apprentices weren't given responsibility for a very important crop until they had proved themselves with the fennel or the parsley, but every crop was important to somebody. A crop of corn was worth tens of thousands of dollars and took up a significant amount of acreage, but someone also needed to keep an eye on the patch of black radishes out behind the barn.

The apprentices also learned a huge amount from my father. His meetings with them could sometimes take hours, involving an intense back-and-forth about some particular crop, a cultivating technique, or a technical problem. My father was concerned about fixing the problem at hand, but he also took his job as a mentor very seriously. He gave them all generous amounts of his time, but sometimes he found a particularly receptive student; other times he gave advice about relationships and living situations and other personal matters. Sometimes he offered advances on paychecks, and he often arranged special accommodations for apprentices who were struggling with issues outside the life of the farm.

On Wednesday afternoons he also held a seminar, at which all the apprentices would gather to discuss some particular issue and ask my father questions. These covered a range of subjects, everything from planning the proper cover crops in the fall to arranging financing for a new piece of equipment. Once a year there would be a slide show about the history of the farm, and he would show old photographs from Sleepy Creek and from the early years on New Morning.

*

When I was little, still young enough to be a kind of mascot to the apprentices, I'd tagged along with them all the time. Back then, in the early eighties, the farm wasn't exactly the same as it was now, and the people who worked there were hippies, minor radicals, stoners. The place sometimes felt more like a summer camp than it did now, and the apprentices got in tomato fights, spent weeks and weeks building tree houses, stayed up late drinking vodka and playing guitar. A little barefoot, grubby blond kid like me was someone to be mothered, or teased, or at least tolerated.

As in any group of people there had also been some odd ones over the years. There was a banjo player who cut off the tips of his fingers in a coffee grinder and a Mennonite who refused to take off her big puffy boots, even when everyone insisted on calling them "moon shoes." There was a muscle-bound guy who had been a stripper and loved to show off how he could make his abs ripple. There was a survivalist who kept fifty-pound sacks of oats and wheat in his cabin. There was a man from Russia who had been a nuclear scientist, drove a Honda with the hood painted as an American flag, and left the farm to work with a particle accelerator at a major research institution.

They lived either on the farm itself or in one of the cottages along the dirt road that my father had purchased over the years, all within walking distance. The quarters on the farm consisted of basic one-room cabins—shacks, really—scattered around the property and lit by kerosene lanterns, without running water or insulation. There was an outhouse behind the barn, with a sign warning about the snakes in the sawdust bin. Most of the apprentices ate in a communal room called the summer kitchen and took showers in an attached room with birds' nests in the rafters. They often listened to the radio in the evenings, or played cards, or just sat on the porch and looked down over the fields.

The aspect that really defined the job, more than the rustic nature of the place, was how far away it was from everything else. The closest movie theater was an hour's drive. There had never been any television reception in the hollow, though a slow and balky Internet connection had been installed in the past year. The wages were low, but there was no place to spend money anyway because the nearest business was in Hustontown, a ten-mile drive, and the only thing to buy there was a stamp at the post office. Getting together to play a game of Scrabble served as a social event.

The crews always developed a personality over a season, and ideally there was a sense of camaraderie, people supporting each other and meshing well, sharing responsibilities. Sometimes there were intense friendships, and almost every summer there were inevitable love affairs. Over the forty years it had been in business, the farm had produced, along with all the vegetables, at least seven marriages and five babies. Lots of these couples had gone on to buy farms of their own, some nearby in Pennsylvania, but also in California and Minnesota and other places.

Sometimes there were conflicts and people felt bitter about how they were being treated. They fought over the normal things: girls, loans, whose turn it was to do the dishes, and more than once those arguments had ended with a minor fistfight out in some distant field. They also sometimes got into arguments with my father, or with the field manager, and then, if the situation couldn't be resolved, they would leave with their last month's pay. It didn't happen often, and not at all in the past year or two, but it was work that tended to attract people who sometimes had trouble being diplomatic.

The crew that summer was better than most because everyone took the work seriously and pulled together. A few of the apprentices had been at the farm for two years or more, and there was a sense of commitment to the farm that encouraged hard and careful work. They were a sober group, but they got obvious satisfaction from doing a job well. If they lacked a sense of irony, some of the prankster spirit that had been part of other crews, they also never missed work because they'd spent the night before drinking home brew and pitching horseshoes until 1:00 a.m. The farm ran more smoothly and efficiently because of it.

✳

After lunch I went back out to the barnyard and told the field manager that I wanted to do some work with the crew.

"Well, we're staking tomatoes in Skunktown," the woman in charge said. "Do you have boots?"

I looked down at my flip-flops.

"I think I have a pair in the house," I said. "Just let me run in and get them."

"We'll wait," she said, "but hurry."

I ran back to the house and found my Red Wings in an upstairs closet, ran back outside, and saw the truck leaving, turning around the corner of the barn and going down the hill. I yelled after it, and someone in the back hit the top of the cab to let the driver know he should stop. One of the dogs started barking like crazy, sure that some calamity was happening. I yelled at him to shut up, caught the truck, and hoisted myself up into the bed. An apprentice shoved some metal stakes out of the way so that I had a space to land. He grinned down at me, a cigarette clenched between his teeth.

"We're going to do some fuckin' farming!" he shouted. We both laughed.

We drove down about a mile to the spread of fields that ran along the far side of the creek until the road made a sharp turn and ended at the edge of the water. The driver never stopped, just drove ahead through the shallow ford while the truck slid a little on the flat slabs of broken shale. I looked down into the water and saw the crayfish scooting away backward and a water snake gliding off in a serene curved line. The truck hit the slope of the opposite bank and reared up over the heavy roots that grew out of the soft dirt and supported the big trees that canted over them at dangerous angles. We came out into the field, the truck dripping, the air smelling like diesel and creek water.

It's easiest to picture the hollow as a wide bowl with a small hill in the center. The Hilltop fields, East and West, were on the very top of that hill, and then below them was the barnyard. On the same level as the barnyard, on a kind of wide terrace, were Behind the Barn, the Garden, and the First, Second, and Third Humps. Below these, laid out in a long curve along the bottom, were the bulk of the fields: the Lower Bottom, the Upper Bottom, the Dogleg, the Far Field, and the End Patch. Extending the curve but on the opposite side of the creek was Skunktown, named for the skunk cabbage that grew in the adjoining swamp, and the farthest from our barnyard was Hortonville, named for a family who had farmed there for a few years.

Skunktown had the most beautiful fields on the farm. They were cut into the grassy flat of the bottom, broken out in the distance by a stand of trees, and lined by foxtail grass and patches of Queen Anne's lace. The tomatoes were planted in low rows, and their tight lines were hemmed on one side by the creek and on the other by a steep piney slope. The whole scene was split down the middle by a simple road, two dusty lines worn in the grass. There was a long view here, one of the only ones on the entire farm, and out in the distance I could see the green ridge run off south, toward the Potomac River some forty miles away.

The tomato crop was still the biggest vegetable at the farm, just like it had been the first summer forty years before. They were planted in successive waves, four generations of them in all, with two thousand plants in each. Staggering them this way had two main purposes: first, it extended the growing season as long as possible, and second, it gave the crop a chance to recover if one generation was ruined by disease or flood. The fields were also spread out all over the farm, with two in the bottom and two up on the Hilltop so that the geography would help protect them from being destroyed all at once. The farm had lost a generation before. In 1996 a huge flood took a huge layer of topsoil and all the tomatoes that were planted in it, but the disaster was reasonably contained and so was the resulting financial loss.

We jumped down off the truck and organized ourselves. The work involved driving metal stakes into the row of plants, one every six feet down the length of the field, so that later someone else could bind the plants with twine and keep them upright. Some of us took hammers and a few stakes, and we all walked out of the shadows under the trees and into the sun. We started hammering, and there was a loud echo of metal striking metal, a sound that started high and thin and got deeper as the stake sunk into the ground. The sun slipped down the ridge as we worked, the shadows going purple.

When we were finished we lay in the weeds off to the side of the tomatoes and lazed around while the pickup came through the grass, made a wide loop around the field, and turned around to take us home. I could feel a lingering vibration in my forearms from all the hammering, and the tips of my fingers prickled and itched. As I looked out at all the stakes standing in the field in long rows, it felt good to see the straight lines of them squared and neat. I looked around at the other people waiting; they were all gazing at the stakes too.

We drove back up to the barnyard and put the tools away. Afterward the apprentices sat around on the walls and in the grass, smoking and talking about the work they'd been doing. Some people had beers and held the cold sweating bottles to their foreheads. I stayed for a few minutes and then left them to walk over to the house. I was a little jealous that I couldn't stay out and drink with them, but someone waved and shouted across the barnyard, "See you in the morning!" I gave a salute and went inside.

＊

Before dinner I washed the blood and rust off my hands at the metal sink in the kitchen. My mother was peeling potatoes, and I put my hands on the cutting board to show her my blisters.

"Ahh, poor baby!," she said, shrugging and lifting up the knife to pretend like she was going to cut off my fingers.

I opened the fridge, stood with the door open, and let the cool air dry the film of sweat off my skin. I found a beer and drank it down in two long swallows.

"Close the fridge door," my mother called from the back porch. She came back into the kitchen with a colander of peas that she'd been snapping. I grinned at her and she grinned back. After a few minutes my father came into the kitchen, got a beer, and sat down across from me at the kitchen table. My mother called in from the porch again, "Jim, take your boots off."

He sighed and undid the laces. He looked around the table, at the peas, the arugula, the kohlrabi. Then he looked at me.

"What happened with the tomatoes?"

"We got them done," I said, happy that he'd asked and that I had an answer.

"Good," he said.

My mother came inside.

"Can we please not talk about vegetables for a minute?"

My father looked at his plate.

"What else should we talk about?"

She came over and sat down, then picked up her fork.

"I don't know, anything. Let's talk about what Arlo's been doing."

"I was staking tomatoes," I said.

After dinner my father went back outside to do some work in his office. My mother and I stayed at the table, talking and picking at the chicken that she'd roasted. Before it got completely dark, we went for a walk down the long slope below the house, past the quiet chicken house where the birds were all sleeping now. A dog came with us and hunted things in the tall grass, jumping on mice that we couldn't see. Our feet crushed the thick plants that grew here, aloes and herbs, and the wet smell of them came drifting up out of the grass as we picked our way down the hill.

We came upon the toppled tree that I'd spotted from the kitchen window that morning. It looked like a whale beached in a meadow. The crown had flattened on one side, forming a hill of leaves thirty feet high. The huge trunk was horizontal, and I climbed up and stood on it. I reached down and pulled my mother up, and we walked along the gentle angle, up into the leaves. We found a nice place to sit, and my mother fumbled around in her pockets and produced a joint. We sat and smoked it, and I lay down and watched the breeze through the leaves. The dog was sitting in the tall grass below, and she barked at us to get our attention.

I had always been close to my mother, but over the summer we would grow much closer. She was willing to relax, to sit out in the grass and talk, would scoff when my father got worked up beyond reason about some small problem that couldn't be fixed anyway. She hadn't always been happy when I was growing up—she used to hide away in an old chicken coop at the bottom of the yard when she wanted to cry—but now we were both old enough to appreciate each other's moods and to realize that parents and children just did the best they could. I thought of her as a confidante, a voice of reason, a goofball who loved making stupid jokes, someone who would spend hours and hours playing Scrabble.

We talked about my sister, Janie, and about a house she was thinking of buying. Janie was four years younger than me and lived in Pittsburgh. I visited her a few weeks after I got home, boarding the train in Huntingdon, where the tracks came through our county on a long arc from New York to Chicago. The trip took me past mile after mile of empty mills before Pittsburgh. She lived in a small house with a wide, flat view of the whole city, the bridges and the brown rivers, and in the distance the tall spire of the Cathedral of Learning at the University of Pittsburgh. Her relationship to the farm in the past few years was like mine, loving but distant, and I didn't see her again until the late fall.

I asked my mother how my father was holding up so far. "Well, he's worried about the tomatoes, but you know your dad." I did know that he could always find a reason to worry. He'd once had a long run of insomnia because he couldn't stop thinking about cabbages, and he listened to the weather radio every morning while he brushed his teeth. There was something specific now though: an alert from the extension office at Penn State saying that they were finding sporadic cases of early blight and that tomato growers should be on notice.

The news wasn't particularly noteworthy, almost definitely nothing to worry about, but the tomatoes were worth a lot of money. Most people bought two or three pounds of them at market on a Saturday morning, enough for a few sandwiches and salads, and at $3.60 a pound that came to about $10. If those $10 were multiplied out over the fifty cases we brought to market, the total came to $4,500, an average tomato sale for a weekend in early September. After all the markets over the season that number grew to around $75,000. We would also sell a small percentage of the tomatoes to the co-op, so the entire crop could generate about $100,000 in sales.

The farm was a cash business, and when my mother emptied the boxes on Monday mornings to count the weekend take, the kitchen smelled strongly of dollar bills. After she was done, after a good market in the high part of the season, she might have $25,000 spread out around her. In the end, when my father holed up in his cold office in December to do the books, the vegetables grown in one season on the farm were worth a little more than half a million dollars. It seemed like a huge amount, way more than anyone could reasonably expect to generate from a piece of land as small as ours.

Once the season was broken down, not much of that money was left for our family. A full 50 percent, half of the expenses of the business, was the labor: paychecks for the apprentices and the few others who worked there. The number of employees shifted with the seasons, as many as twenty-five at the height of the summer and just two or three in January, but even in the depths of winter, when the work shifted to snowplowing, tasks in the greenhouse, and crop planning for the next season, there were always people to be paid.

There were plenty of claims to the rest of the money. There was hardware, rolls of chicken wire, PVC pipe, five-gallon buckets of red paint for the sheds and outbuildings. There was equipment, basic things like new cultivator tines and more elaborate purchases like a specialized potato digger imported from Italy. Money kept all those machines running smoothly and filled the gas pump on the farm. The markets also cost a lot to run: paper bags, tables, scales, and calculators, fuel for the trucks. In the winter there was a big payment for seeds for the following spring.

The farm had narrow margins, and in the end my parents only saw about 10 percent of the farm's vegetables in profit. The number had drifted up in the last ten years, but it had always been a middle-class wage. In most ways this meant that I'd had a normal kind of childhood as part of a small business, like having a father who ran a garage, or being part of a dry cleaning business, or living above a funeral home. There was a basic frugality; my parents had one car, a Camry that they kept for years, and when it finally gave out they bought another one, but there had always been money for new shoes, regular dentist visits, and food on the table.

There was always anxiety too. The farm was susceptible to huge financial swings, and those bad years, ones when the farm was a total loss, loomed large. The summer between my year in first grade and second there had been a bad drought in Pennsylvania. The farm didn't have any irrigation, almost all the crops had died, and all the apprentices had left because there was no work. In 1987 there was a hurricane, and in the mid-nineties, when I had been away at boarding school, a series of floods had destroyed the bottom fields. It was only a few years later, when I found an essay that my mother had written and left in a bottom drawer of her desk, that I realized how close we'd come to losing everything.

The threat from the weather never went away. The worst-case scenario, a season when it rained every single day, or weekly hailstorms or a plague of locusts, was unlikely, and even if all the crops had been wiped out, an entire season gone, the farm would probably be able to limp into the next year and try to recoup its losses. Two bad years though, combined with some event like a fire or a significant injury, would be harder to recover from. A farm the size of ours couldn't afford crop insurance, and there were no government subsidies or assistance. Those programs were designed for farms on a much different scale than ours, operations that grew many thousands of acres of one crop and produced much higher revenues. It was one thing to apply a formula to quantify the failure of five thousand acres of wheat, and another to understand a flood that might destroy six small patches of different vegetables, a manure spreader, a pile of irrigation pipe, and a layer of topsoil that had been developed over a decade. Even navigating the bureaucracy would have been a full-time job.

My father had never been a farmer just on principle, and even on that first patch of land in Sleepy Creek he'd intended to make his living by growing vegetables. There were no good models available for making a living that way, and so he'd had to be creative and take risks with money that he couldn't always afford. He felt the bad weather and the diseases not as events beyond his control but as repudiations of the system he'd developed. His livelihood, and the sense that he'd made it on his own, was one of his proudest achievements, but he also took the failures personally.

I was proud of the fact that my parents were willing to live with so much uncertainty. I had lived in Manhattan for five years, and then in Cambridge, and so I understood how money worked—what it bought and also what it meant. I knew that money could offer safety and solace, and to deny its importance was silly, and that everyone in the world, whether they fought against the feeling or not, liked to hold it in their hands. By the time I was thirty and still didn't have a savings account, I was also starting to understand the unassailable truth that money was the only way to really be a part of the world. You didn't have to have a lot of it, but you had to have it.

3

This summer wasn't the very first time that I'd left a city and come back to the farm. Six years before, I had left my job in Manhattan and come back to Pennsylvania for what I thought would be a short visit but had ended up lasting almost a year. I had lived in the city for a little more than five years altogether at that point, during the first half of the aughts, and I'd always enjoyed it. I lived there during a summer in college, and I'd come back after graduating, part of the annual wave of new arrivals. The city was booming during those years, and I was a happy participant. Someone once threw a battery at me from the projects on Avenue C, but that was the worst I got of the old, bad New York.

My first job in New York, between my junior and senior years, was an internship in the Queens County public defenders office. The work consisted of driving around the far reaches

of the borough, visiting the scenes of petty crimes, and trying to talk to people who might exonerate our clients. My
partner and I, a boy from Rochester, blindingly white and
plump, would climb the dark stairwells of projects in Far
Rockaway or knock on the doors of tiny ranch houses next to
LaGuardia Airport and try to interview witnesses. We were
rarely successful, but we were so obviously harmless that it
never seemed to occur to anyone to threaten us.

After moving back to the city after college, I'd left again
to go to Australia for a few months. I wanted to travel, and I
knew that the country offered work visas for American back-
packers, so I figured I could make some money there while I
moved around. The hostels advertised jobs, most of them for
temporary work on farms and orchards, so I supported myself
by trimming apple trees outside of Gundagai and picking green
peaches near Boorowa. The longest stint was a job on a planta-
tion near Yungaburra where I worked in water up to my thighs,
cutting banana trees down with a machete and killing the roots
by injecting them with kerosene from a tank I carried on my
back. At first it was a strange adventure, but then those dusty
farm towns in Australia—each with one pub and a fight out
front every Saturday night—started to seem boring, and the
jobs felt a lot like what I could be doing back home on the
farm in Pennsylvania. I was tired of working so hard, and I was
desperate to get back to New York, where I could find a job
that involved sitting at a desk all day.

I came back to New York as thin as a rail, tanned and
bleached, and slept on the couch of the friend who had kept
my stuff. I lived on my credit cards, and eventually a friend

from college left his job as a paralegal at a law firm and offered me his position. I worked on the deal to approve the Verizon signage on a building on Fifty-Ninth Street and helped close the sale of three airplanes to the Turkish government. After the firm's Christmas party I slept with the soft redhead from Oklahoma who sat in the cubicle behind me.

Eventually I left the law firm and found a job working at a literary agency. The monolith of the Empire State Building watched over the neighborhood, and down below my office window the Senegalese peddlers on Broadway sold flip-flops by the gross. My boss was impossibly charming; his hair was perfectly tousled, the frames of his glasses were the exact right shade of tortoiseshell, and his blazer was precisely tailored. He looked like the most dangerous boy in the senior class of an elite prep school.

In those years I saw all kinds of beautiful and terrible things: protesters at the Republican National Convention facing down the endless phalanxes of horse-mounted police in the dark streets; the *Queen Mary* 2 suddenly filling the canyon of West Thirty-Fourth Street and blotting out the sunset over New Jersey; the lines of dusty people walking uptown after 9/11.

And I had fun too. I had a drug dealer named Earl the Pearl who would bring me cocaine at odd hours, and I had scars on the palms of my hands from drinking bottles of Black Label, then climbing over the rusty fences that blocked off the crumbling esplanade along the East River.

The blackout of 2003 was my last great memory of New York. It happened on a Thursday, and once my colleagues and I had asked around and decided that it probably wasn't terrorism, we filed out into the streets and walked home. I went to my apartment on Second Street and Avenue B and groped my way up the pitch-black stairwell to get a flashlight and a bottle of whiskey. By ten o'clock someone had lit the trash cans on fire in Tompkins Square Park, and people danced under the trees. We bought beer before the coolers in delis went warm, and the restaurants along Avenue A gave away their melting ice cream. We sat in the dark at the sidewalk cafés and drank our beer and smoked joints. Late at night we walked uptown, and the buildings made endless dark miles of towering blank cliffs, the stars visible at the tops of the canyons.

Eventually my job ended when my boss stopped showing up to work. We hadn't seen him for days, until one Monday morning we found empty beer bottles in our trash cans and a crack pipe in a desk drawer. There were burn marks on the bookcases where someone had set down the pieces of hot glass. Just a few days later he was dragged out by force from the hotel where he had been staying and was committed to a hospital, the financial affairs were wound down, and one Tuesday we put all the leftover furniture in a storage unit on Grand Street and the business was officially closed. We all felt betrayed, and silly for being fooled so easily by the addict in our office, but it was also exciting to be a close witness to such a sordid drama. I was now the owner of an epic story and, even better, I was the blameless victim, free to bask in reflected notoriety. I was also eligible for six months of unemployment checks.

I'd lost my job, but I wasn't done with New York. I had one last chance to stay in Manhattan and I blew it. After the agency closed, I'd wrangled an interview with a man at Condé Nast, someone whose name appeared on multiple mastheads. When he came to the reception desk, one of his eyes was red with a burst vessel, and it was hard to know where to look. At the end of the interview, I misjudged the layout of the office and went to the window to have a peek at the long view down to Times Square. I realized too late that I'd made the mistake of walking behind his desk. When I turned around, I knew that I had seemed too familiar, hadn't known my place, and that I wouldn't get the job.

I hadn't thought very much about why I'd wanted to move to New York after college because it had just seemed like the inevitable place to go. I'd gone to Cornell, and most of my friends moved to the city also, and for the first few years we formed a happy, drunken little band. I'd spent time there before; my family had visited often when I was growing up, staying with an aunt who lived on West Eighty-First Street. I'd been to the Macy's Thanksgiving Day Parade, and to the East Village, had seen *The Nutcracker* at Lincoln Center, and spent hours in Zabar's with my dad as he asked the men behind the counter innumerable questions about the food they were selling.

It wasn't until I was about to leave that I understood how much I had invested myself in the city. I'd grown up on the farm, but I never thought that my life would have meaning there; it was my parents' project, and I was just a bystander. Living in New York was a chance to feel important. For me, at the age of twenty-six, success seemed like a matter of dazzling a room, getting the inside tip, delivering the perfect pitch, and I was sure that I was in the right place at the right time. I had watched my boss at parties, listened to him on the phone, paid close attention to how he dressed, the tricks to being powerful and respected. It would take years more for me to understand that there was no magic involved and that it was mostly a matter of hard work, no matter where I lived.

My mother came to New York and drove me back to Pennsylvania. Somewhere on the New Jersey Turnpike I told her that my life was over. Everything that could possibly matter would happen within the twenty-five square miles of Manhattan, and everything outside them, including the acres of the farm, was completely pointless. If I were older, or less self-centered, or just more sensitive, I would have realized how much that would hurt her feelings.

*

On my second day back at the farm after driving home from Massachusetts, I joined the crew at 8:00, the normal start time. The apprentices were happy for the extra set of hands, and I knew the basics of most of the jobs, so they didn't need to babysit me too much. We picked red oak lettuce first thing, before the sun burned off the fog and it got too hot, and then I moved some sacks of oyster shell down to the chicken house and helped place thin trays of basil in the greenhouse. After lunch we went down to Skunktown to finish staking the tomatoes. The next day was similar, and the day after that, and pretty soon I was used to being home and working with the crew. After just two weeks, eating plenty of vegetables and working outside all day, I felt thin and healthy, and I was sleeping well at night.

✳

The decor in our house had always been heavy on images of fruits and vegetables. Vintage tomato labels hung on the wall by the door in the kitchen, and there was a watercolor of a woman selling carrots under the wall clock. Next to the sink there was a pastel of a single ripe mango. The only picture in the kitchen that didn't feature a fruit or a vegetable was a framed funeral announcement, a black-and-white photograph of a farmer sitting on a tractor smiling at the camera.

The picture was of a man named Bert DeLeeuw, a fellow farmer and friend of my parents' who had been murdered twenty years before. He had come to Pennsylvania to start a farm of his own and then five years later had been shot to death by his neighbor while planting zucchini on an early spring evening. The facts of this murder weren't complicated, and almost none of them were under dispute because the crime had been carried out in full daylight and in close view of three witnesses. The man who committed the crime was a retired postal worker named George William Robb, sixty-nine years old and a lifetime resident of Huntingdon County. The argument that precipitated the killing was about Bert's dogs and how they had been scaring some horses that Robb kept on an adjoining property. There were three eyewitnesses to the murder, including Bert's wife, Lina, and Robb eventually pled guilty to a charge of third-degree murder. He was an old man, and an alcoholic, and he may have been permitted to such a reduced charge because of his age and declining health.

Bert had been shot when I was twelve years old, and I remembered the crime as one of the most intense events of my childhood. I was old enough then to know all the details and to understand that the murder had been a senseless act. I hadn't forgotten what had happened by the time I came home twenty years later, but the details were worn smooth. The circumstances had been dramatic, and it was a very big deal for our family at the time—when I was twelve years old I remembered feeling like it was the most important thing that had ever happened to any of us—but eventually it stopped seeming so extraordinary. It became a little piece of history, tragic but only occasionally remembered.

Bert had been one of my father's best friends. They had originally met in Washington, part of the same large group of acquaintances, and Bert moved to Pennsylvania with Lina in 1986, ten years after my parents. At the time of his death their farm was still struggling, but it was an operating business and it was getting stronger. He and Lina had one child together, a girl named Chloe, and they had fixed up an old farmhouse and made it comfortable. He had a solid piece of farmland with room for expansion, the basic set of equipment, and a growing market to sell what he was producing. He had also been one of the earliest and most enthusiastic proponents of the farmers' co-op. He had worked hard on that project with my father, and even if it hadn't yet started to thrive by the time he was killed, Bert had been essential to the early makeup of the organization.

What was interesting about Bert, what set him apart from many of the other farmers that were doing similar things, was his mythmaking impulse. One person might post a to-do list by the door to focus himself on the tasks at hand, but Bert hung a woodcut of John Henry—the steel-driving man—on his kitchen wall, where he would see it when he made his coffee. Another farmer might dig a well for irrigation, but Bert dug a huge pond instead, floated a boat there, and stocked the water full of fat bass. Another citizen might write a letter to the editor about his issues with a nearby dump, but Bert built huge papier-mâché puppets, vultures with wingspans forty feet across, and marched with them in the local parade, right behind the homecoming queen in her shiny pickup. Some people might get together for a potluck and a keg, but Bert organized a square dance instead, complete with a caller, a mandolin, and two people on banjo, and when it was over, he built a massive bonfire, and after that burned down, he took everyone up to the hilltop above the farm to see the fireflies and the stars. He shaved with a straight razor, he kept a fancy chess set, he divorced one smart, beautiful woman and married another. To the twelve-year-old boy I was then, and maybe also to the thirty-one-year-old man I was now, it was easy to think about a person like Bert as some kind of hero.

One night, a week or two after I got home, we finished with dinner and were sitting around the table drinking coffee. I mentioned the funeral announcement, just in passing, that hung on the wall behind my father's place at the table, the photo of Bert on a tractor, his dates of birth and death below. My father looked down at his plate and pushed around the bone from his pork chop.

"Why are you interested?"

"I don't know, just curious. It's been up there a long time."

He put his cup down. Then he put his hand over his eyes and made one deep sobbing sound, his body clenching around the noise almost like a violent sneeze. Then he picked his cup back up and continued to drink his coffee like nothing had happened.

My mother and I both waited for him to say something else. After a few more seconds he shook his head and apologized. He seemed surprised himself, and a little embarrassed, but then he brushed it off and said that he felt better, and so we started talking about the green beans and whether two of the apprentices were secretly sharing a cabin. My mother put away the extra vegetables and threw the pork bones out the front door where the dogs were waiting patiently. My father nodded off while he finished his coffee, resting his chin on his chest and snoring lightly, until he suddenly woke with a start and went out to finish writing invoices in his office.

My father and Bert had been close colleagues. They had stayed up late together arguing about the best size flat for planting lettuce seeds, the merits of a fancy piece of equipment for seeding corn, the wisdom of trying to get an early jump on the warm weather and putting a field of squash seedlings at risk. They had fun together, meeting at the M&M Diner—the restaurant that Bert claimed was the best in the county—and playing tennis together on Sundays at the old forgotten tennis courts behind the high school in Pogue. As two men in the prime of life, they could also be competitive. My father may have been a little in awe of Bert's charisma, and Bert may have been a bit jealous of my father's experience.

My father was more reserved, wary of the huge romantic gesture. Bert was impatient and less willing to worry over the small details. Most importantly though they shared an essential mission: farming as a special kind of calling. I think part of why my father cried that evening was because the reminder of Bert's death had touched some deep well of feeling, something that was always present but often forgotten in the daily running of the farm.

✳

My father started New Morning Farm because he had tried other jobs and none of them felt as fulfilling as he had hoped. It was a long process though, and a lot had happened before my grandparents put up four thousand dollars—a significant sum in 1972 for a middle-class family like theirs—so that their thirty-two-year-old son could try and be a farmer. My grandmother was an English teacher. She grew up in Idaho, and my grandfather worked in a printing plant. Neither of them came from a farming background. This desire to grow vegetables must have seemed slightly ridiculous to them, living a comfortable suburban life with all the modern conveniences, where cake came from a mix and carrots from a can. But they did remember that when he was only eight years old, my father dug up their entire yard to plant cucumbers and tomatoes. I guess the farm wasn't entirely unexpected.

In the late 1940s, places like Norwood, Massachusetts, the town where my father grew up, still had a few farms out around the edges, and once a week in the summer a farmer drove a horse-drawn wagon down the street and sold vegetables from the back. When my father was a little boy, he was obsessed with this, and he begged the farmer to give him a job. He was turned down, so he started the little patch in the backyard instead. These were the vegetables that he sold from his red wagon, and he stuck with it for years. Eventually he fell in love with sailing, so he stopped spending time in the patch, but he didn't forget how much he had always enjoyed it.

He joined the United States Navy when he was a junior in high school, mostly because he loved boats and the navy would let him sail. It wasn't an obvious choice for him, but the navy offered to pay for college at Rice University in Houston, Texas, and service to country had a certain attraction for a boy growing up with President Kennedy's words about a "New Frontier" echoing in his ears. He was an ROTC candidate, and if he enjoyed the navy at first—or at least didn't mind it too much—that changed in 1965, when he was sent away during spring break to Camp Pendleton in Southern California to train with the marines. As a way of toughening up the soft navy boys—the officers working toward their college degrees—the marines organized a simulated battlefield and called in heavy air support. Any sort of subtlety about what the navy was about—the abstract pleasures of charting courses on maps or calculating engine speeds under heavy load—suddenly drained out of my father. He realized that he might be about to go to Vietnam, where he would be asked to kill people for reasons that weren't entirely clear to him.

When he got back to Rice in the fall, he was certain that he would become a conscientious objector, even if it put his scholarship at risk. One of his professors of philosophy—a man who gave exciting lectures about existentialism—helped him to embrace this choice, while another professor, a career officer from Harvard, made arguments for the fraternity of the military and the opportunity to serve a just cause. The professor and the officer each wrote my father letters explaining their respective positions, and for a senior in college it must have seemed incredibly heady and romantic. In the end though, he stuck with the navy, with Henry V and the heroics of "once more unto the breach," instead of the lonely uncertainty of a man without a country. He was assigned to his first commission in June 1964 on the USS *Northampton*, a cruiser known as the Floating White House, a ship kept constantly afloat to receive the president in case of nuclear attack. While my father was serving, Lyndon Johnson came on board— with Lady Bird in his wake—to review the accommodations and to see if the bed was large enough to fit his six-foot, four-inch frame.

After his posting on the *Northampton*, he was asked to attend training at the Defense Language Institute in Monterey, California, to learn Russian. He spent a year in intensive study, and his test scores were the highest in his class. The last part of his training though was an application for top-secret clearance. He couldn't do his work without it. An FBI agent with a thick folder sat him down and asked him questions about his earlier struggles with the idea of being a conscientious objector. Eventually his clearance was denied, and he went to Vietnam that fall.

The thing my father remembers most about the war was the feeling of uncertainty. The 17th parallel was demarcated in 1954 to divide North and South Vietnam, but it was impossible to know who was on the right side. His task was to convince skeptical populations of the American position. Mostly he helped villagers out of jams and delivered mess hall scraps for their pigs. The people were happy to take what was offered, but there was a pervasive sense of danger and constant rumors of subversion. A sailor under his command got jumpy and killed an old man. A Vietnamese boy fell from a truck and was crushed. A soldier was shot on patrol; later it was determined that he had been murdered. Rockets and bombs whistled into the base without any warning.

When he returned from the war, things in Washington had changed. Johnson had declared an end to the bombing in Vietnam, and soon Nixon would take over the White House. That fall, my father learned of the first officer who had publicly criticized the war. Suddenly opposition that had previously been vague and undefined was organized into structures. Organizations like Vietnam Veterans Against the War sprung up, Eugene McCarthy looked like a viable antiwar candidate for president, and soon John Kerry would testify in front of Congress and wonder publicly about the last man who would be asked to die in Vietnam. My father helped to form the Concerned Officers Movement, a group of soldiers in leadership positions who publicly questioned the wisdom of their superiors. After Nixon ordered the expansion of the war into Cambodia in 1970, my father resigned in protest from the United States Navy. If he had stayed in, he would have been honorably discharged two weeks later.

He left for Russia just a month or two later on a cultural

exchange trip that he'd heard about through connections he had made in language school. He traveled with a group of Georgetown University students, taking the train from Helsinki during the White Nights. In his dorm room in Leningrad he sat and bullshitted with other Russians his age and discussed big ideas. He came back to Washington that winter and met friends he'd made through the Concerned Officers Movement and other organizations, feeling out his connections and trying to find a job where he could work against the war. Someone introduced him to Marty Peretz, a professor at Harvard who would soon become the publisher of *The New Republic*, and his wife, Anne, who was an heir to the Singer Sewing Machine fortune. Peretz invited him to dinner in Cambridge to discuss working for them. Eventually they arranged a job for him in the office of Bella Abzug, a congresswoman from New York and one of the most outspoken and prominent figures in the antiwar movement.

In his role as a military caseworker, he mostly wrote letters in support of other soldiers who were questioning the war. There were airmen who were being punished for publishing op-eds, officers who were refused a discharge on grounds of conscientious objection, sailors who wanted to speak at protests but had been denied leave. In the fall, he enrolled in law school so that he could better understand the rules of the game and learn to be an agent of change from within.

He and his friends rented the house in Sleepy Creek, a place to spend quiet weekends away from Washington. My father planted a garden and tended it, a few tomato plants and a little spinach. He was surprised to see how much produce he actually ended up with, too much for him to eat alone, so he harvested the vegetables and took them back to DC. One day in September, the season over and the leaves turned brown, he loaded up his car and drove to law school. He got all the way to campus before deciding to drive back to Sleepy Creek and stay.

✳

When I was four years old, before I started school and needed to follow a routine, my parents still took me along sometimes when they hung out in Washington after market day on Saturday. Some of their friends were the same people who had rented the house in Sleepy Creek ten years before in the early seventies, and these people had since graduated from law school and started jobs at law firms, nonprofits, or government agencies. I remembered sips of beer from bottles offered by friendly adults and being put to bed on a couch while my mother lay with me and sang until I fell asleep and she could go back to the party. Bert hadn't known my parents previously, but a friend of my father introduced them, and they came to be friends. Bert invited them to the dinners he held in his apartment on T Street and offered a place to crash when they were in DC. I remembered Bert in his apartment on the top floor of an old row house, laughing and turning up the record player, eating strawberries my parents had brought over, arguing about Ronald Reagan.

Sometimes I stayed with Bert on Saturday mornings while

my parents were selling vegetables in the city. I'd ride around with him while he did errands, or we'd go to the zoo, and once he took me to an Orioles game in the old concrete stadium outside of Baltimore. One of my strongest memories was of him buying me a lottery ticket at a 7-Eleven on T Street. Even today, decades later, I can remember that morning very clearly: the thin African cashier, the feeling of scratching off the soft gray box with a quarter, and how excited he was when, against all odds, I won a hundred dollars.

When I was a little kid, I knew that Bert talked to the black people in his neighborhood even though they didn't expect him to, and I'd seen a picture of him being arrested by the police even though my parents told me that he hadn't done anything wrong. I knew that my mother had a button that she'd kept in a box on her bureau from Bert's wedding that said "Legalize Bert and Madeline," and that this was funny for some reason that only adults could understand. I knew that Bert had big parties at his house and that everyone from the neighborhood came to drink beer and talk about Latin America and nuclear weapons.

When I was older, after he'd moved to Pennsylvania, I knew that Bert had been appointed to fill an unexpired term as Walker Township supervisor. I wasn't sure how he pulled it off, considering that Huntingdon County was one of the most conservative counties in Pennsylvania, and he'd only lived there for three years, but I assumed that his natural charisma overcame a lot of misgivings, that his ability to get things done must have been apparent. He had a bumper sticker on his white Nissan pickup truck that I still remembered: "Robin Hood Was Right."

I didn't know until I was an adult how involved Bert was in national politics, and that he was a kind of freelance organizer and provocateur. His obituary, published in the *New York Times* on May 6, 1990, noted that in 1968 he'd helped organize demonstrations for welfare rights and that later he was an official of the National Welfare Rights Organization. He'd worked in the presidential campaigns of Senator George McGovern, Senator Fred Harris, and Barry Commoner. In another picture of him being arrested during those years, he was sitting on the ground with a hand on each knee, a calm expression on his face as he was dragged toward a paddy wagon by the scruff of the neck.

I was eight years old when Bert decided to leave Washington and move to Pennsylvania with his new partner, Lina, an artist, to start a farm and grow vegetables like my parents. The first few times we went over to Blue Moon Farm it was still a rough operation; the house was old, the outbuildings were falling down, and the fields were oddly placed. They were in the process then of fixing things up, making the house livable and the fields more productive. More than my parents, Bert and Lina also thought about the aesthetics of their farm, how it felt to drive in and see the fields along the creek and the house up on its hill.

In the picture on his funeral announcement Bert was wearing a plaid shirt and his pants were held up with suspenders. He had on a straw hat, a neat fedora with a black band. He had a bushy mustache and wire-framed glasses, and he was sitting on the seat of a Model M Farmall and smiling down at the camera. He looked healthy and his eyes were sparkling. There was a poem by Wendell Berry printed below the picture, a verse about farming as a spiritual practice with a final line that noted a "willing descent into the grass."

What came through most clearly in that portrait was how confident Bert looked on his tractor. It was easy to forget that he was just a guy from the city, someone with almost no farming experience, a person who was just barely making a living. If he was worried about Blue Moon, about his ability to make it work, none of that came through in the photograph. He looked like he fit in, like he belonged there, and it would take me years to understand how rare and important that kind of confidence was.

His enthusiasm was also infectious. My father once told me how excited he had been when Bert started Blue Moon. "He was just different. Everyone knew it," my father said. "He had something about him, some kind of confidence that drew people to him." I could tell that he was still somewhat mystified by Bert's ability to embrace things so wholeheartedly, and he was surprised even years later by the powerful attraction of that personality. As the conversation wound down, there was a moment of silence. Then my father looked me in the eye and said, "When Bert decided to be a farmer, it was the most important compliment I've ever gotten."

✳

A few days after the incident with my father at the dinner table, I decided to drive up north and see the acres where

Bert had lived and died. I hadn't been to Blue Moon Farm since I was twelve years old, but I remembered that there was a big square farmhouse built from rough-hewn logs and chinked with lime, that the fields stretched out in a shallow valley between two grassy hills, that the property was split by a small stream that ran out of the wooded ridges to the north. I remembered being excited to go there when I was little because it was usually for a potluck or some kind of party, and I also remembered the last time I could truly recall being there, which was the day of Bert's funeral.

I drove my father's truck up to Blue Moon, out the dirt road and north toward the county seat. The drive was pretty bleak, through the old coal and railroad towns in this part of the state. I went through Burnt Cabins, where I once saw a rat steal a Hershey bar from behind the taps of the local bar; Mapleton, with a sand plant that was still limping along; and Mount Union, where half the town got laid off after the brick factory closed. It had never been a particularly prosperous county to begin with, and the last few decades hadn't been getting much better.

I drove past the prison, found the turnoff to the left, and went out into the network of winding roads for another few miles until I saw the dirt track on the right that led to Blue Moon. The road ran up a tight wooded valley, dark and shaded, and after a half mile I came out of the trees and saw the fields to my right. There was a tall hill grown up with high green grass, and in the distance was the barn and the house. Down below was the pond, flat and gray in the sunlight, and some old machinery rusting in a damp swale filled with jewel weed.

I parked the truck in the barnyard and got out to look around. No one seemed to be home, but I knew that people were living there, a doctor from the hospital in town and his wife, who had bought the place from Lina. The wife was a blacksmith, and they had built a house and a kiln on the other side of the pond. The fields didn't look like they were being farmed, and I didn't feel comfortable walking in them without permission. I left the truck in a conspicuous enough place so I wouldn't surprise anyone.

I walked up to the barn and slipped into the building through the crack between the sliding doors. Everything inside was under tarps, big dull shapes that loomed in the half dark. An old hay hook was suspended from the rafters on the end of a chain, and there were bright white pinprick holes in the tin roof. Something scurried along one of the old crossbeams, and the pigeons in the rafters cooed.

It was a sturdy barn and still pretty much the way I had remembered it. It had accommodated different farmers in the last sixty or eighty years, and it could probably be useful for another hundred years to come. My eyes adjusted slowly, and I walked around, the wide floorboards flexing under my feet. Someone had tacked up old license plates on one of the side walls, lined up in order of the expiration dates. The oldest ones were from the 1920s and used the antique "Penna" abbreviation, but the last one in the row of them was Bert's: a red, white, and blue plate from Washington, DC, that said "Nation's Capital."

I was happy to see that little bit of Bert there in the murky half-light. When I'd been here as a child the farm was always busy—a building going up, a pond being dug, a field being plowed—but I'd been away so long, and my memories now were so clouded by the murder, that the place felt frozen in that sad time. It felt solemn and heartbreaking: the sun cutting through the slats of the old barn, the tiger lilies nodding in the breeze, the stillness of the empty fields.

Bert's funeral, held in this same barn, was a potluck, just like all the other parties at Blue Moon. The young farmers brought covered dishes made from the vegetables they had in the freezer, and some of them wore clean denim and their boots. They looked like they might be able to go right back to work when they got home. Some of the women wore dresses they'd sewed themselves that showed off their tan muscled arms and their downy legs. A family of musicians played violins and a harp, and someone picked a banjo.

Those old bluegrass tunes and folk ballads—songs originally recorded on scratchy wax records, written down on ragged sheet music, first played by men in flat-brim hats who stared out from old daguerreotypes—were hymns to agriculture. The subjects of those songs were brothers gone to war and cornfields left untended, grieving wives drowned in slow rivers, fathers in graves grown over with wild roses. And now it felt like Bert, this improbable farmer, had somehow managed to write one of those songs for himself.

They used the middle bay of the barn for the service, the largest available space—swept the floor, moved the machinery out, and set up folding metal chairs in rows. There was a small door in the back wall, designed to allow hay to be thrown down from the loft, and it opened out into a long view of the pond and the hills. The chairs faced toward the door so that everyone could see the fields, and the speakers stood in the bright light to read their passages and reflections. I don't remember any arrangements of flowers or other decorations, and there was no body.

Someone had spoken about what a skilled carpenter Bert had been, and someone else discussed his talents as a sailor. I remember my father speaking and having to pause and collect himself a few times. He mostly discussed what a good tennis player Bert was and how he'd practiced against a backboard for hours and hours, doing the steady, lonely, repetitive work of perfecting his forehand. I remember it as a eulogy about how stubborn he was and how much he cared about getting things right.

*

I walked out of the barn into the full sun. To the right was a small brook, with saplings and marshy plants growing along its banks, and an old springhouse, a small rectangular building with no windows. It had been built for refrigeration originally, and when I stepped inside I saw the pool of cold water, captured from the spring, which glimmered in the dim light and absorbed the scuffling sounds of my feet. I reached down and ran my fingers over the smooth surface; tiny waves finned away from me, the water glinting like it was full of minnows. I watched tadpoles dart in the cold cistern for a long second, remembering how Bert had floated bottles of beer here during his parties.

After a few moments enjoying the cool dark, I went and had a look at the wood and glass greenhouse that Bert and Lina had bought from an old man nearby, and then I walked up to the farmhouse on the hill behind me. It was heavy, stockade-like, built from huge logs that interlocked at the corners. There was a kitchen on the right, a glassed-in porch, front steps paved with stones from the creek, and a handrail fashioned from a long, smooth tree limb.

Even now I could tell that the house would have been a difficult place to live. Bert and Lina lived there for four years but it always felt forbiddingly homespun. The rooms were still mostly unfinished when Bert died, and I remembered sneaking away during a party to wander around the halls where the mud dauber wasps had built their clay nests. Behind the house was a studio that Bert had built for Lina, and still hanging there was a little blue crescent moon painted with yellow letters: Blue Moon Farm.

I hacked my way through the milkweed below the barn to an old Ford truck with a short bed and bubble-shaped fenders. It was the truck that Bert and Lina used to drive to the farmers' market in town, the dark-green paint rubbed shiny and the back always full of vegetables. A few feet away sat his tractor, the nubs of its massive black wheels sinking in the mud. My father had found this tractor for Bert, had asked around until he found an old man looking to unload one for cheap. It was almost the same model as ours and in the same red color that all International tractors were painted. It was also the tractor from Bert's funeral announcement photo, his arm thrown over the wheel. Except for the rust, it looked the same as it did in the picture, exposed and spare, like something flayed.

Before I left Blue Moon that afternoon I had the urge to walk down and see the place where Bert had actually been shot. I left the tractor and the old truck and walked into the field along the road. A flock of white moths came up out of the grass, and I couldn't help but think of ghosts. Somewhere on this narrow field his blood had soaked into the green grass. They'd spread Bert's ashes there a few weeks later, the gray dust whipping in the wind, catching in the tall grass and sprinkling the surface of the pond.

I knew that I was being dramatic now, even just giving myself a thrill, but I'd often felt a particular sense of dread in Pennsylvania. I had been a fearful kid, scared of the sound of the whip-poor-will as it got dark, worried about strangers coming out of the woods. To help me sleep I was allowed to keep a Civil War sword in my bed. It had been my great-great-grandfather's, and on its hilt was the engraving "Presented by his men to E. C. Crawford, Roxbury, Massachusetts." Every night I had lain beside it, scared of the dark, and felt the cool brass against my leg.

After Bert died, Lina tried to stay on the farm. People came to stay there with her, and they helped to keep things busy, but she needed to go into town, where there were other people. It didn't help that everything had happened so close to the house and that the family of the man who killed Bert was living right down the road, and that the dogs were still there, wagging their tails and asking to be fed, or that the seat of the pickup truck was still stained with blood, or that the squash they'd been planting when it happened was still growing in the field.

My father once told me that Bert's murder was a freak event, more like getting hit by lightning than a story with a logical conclusion. I knew that he was partly right, but I also knew that Bert's ambition and personality had been part of the story too. If he hadn't been brave enough to go out to the middle of nowhere and start a farm, and to be optimistic about his chances, then he wouldn't have been out in the field that day when his neighbor showed up with his shotgun and his grievances.

I got back in the truck and turned the key in the ignition. The radio suddenly blared out, and I quickly shut it off, embarrassed, though there was no one around. I drove down the long driveway and passed the farmhouse where William Robb had lived. I kept going until I was on the hard road. Eventually I came out of the valley and went back past the prison, the ice factory, and the fairgrounds and into town.

※

The winter before this, when I was home from Massachusetts visiting my parents for the holidays, I'd gone to visit another old farm. It was a few days before Christmas, and I asked my father if we could drive down to see the place in Sleepy Creek where he'd first started growing vegetables. It wasn't far away but I'd never been there before, and I don't know what I expected to see. Some empty fields, an old house, maybe an old shed he'd built. Even if we didn't see much of anything, it would be a nice way to spend a few hours together.

We drove through McConnellsburg and down the line of the ridge to Sleepy Creek, through the typical midwinter landscape of spare trees, mown hills, and slushy mud. As we drove my father talked about how it had felt to come there for that first summer, and about girlfriends I'd never heard of and projects I'd never seen. It was late afternoon when we came into Hancock, the biggest town in the area, and the sun had mostly gone down behind the ridges. The Potomac River marked the Mason-Dixon Line in this part of Maryland, and historical markers along the way noted the location of temporary field hospitals during the Civil War.

Most of the stores in town were empty. The businesses that were still open were mostly in repurposed buildings: the hand-painted sign of the Grocery Box was nailed on what looked like an old Dairy Queen; the Triangle Bar was built into the parlor of an old wooden frame house. The few people on the street were either very old and wearing feed caps or very young and wearing oversized sports jerseys. We drove by an old building, now cut up into apartments, with the word "Bank" carved into the stone above the door. My father pointed it out and mentioned that he'd gone there to get his first loan, backed by a certificate of deposit from his parents, money he used to buy a pickup truck.

From Hancock we drove over a bridge, and the road suddenly got narrow again. The route we were following dipped under the highway and then ran along the river; on one side the woods climbed right up the ridge, and on the other the land spread out along the bottom where the cornstalks lay down in the mud. The Potomac rolled slow and opaque, looking especially dangerous in the cold. The distant glint and whine of Route 70 on the other side of the river made the fields seem even lonelier. We crossed a one-lane bridge and saw a few old houses clustered around a bend in the road: the village of Sleepy Creek.

On the left was a sign that said: "Sleepy Creek Campground. Private." We pulled onto the dirt lane and over the hump of a raised railroad track and past a few idled boxcars on a short siding. An old black Ford pickup came out of the field beyond. There were three boys in the front, the smallest one sitting in the middle, where he'd have to straddle the stick shift. It was cold, but the boys were shirtless and whippet-thin, their white chests slightly concave. They looked dully at us, and one of them gave the little wave that involves lifting two fingers off the steering wheel. My father lifted his two fingers in turn.

Spread out in front of us we could see about seventy-five old travel trailers in varying states of repair, set down along the river. As much as possible, they looked secured for the winter. The only other structure was an abandoned house that sat on the ridge looking over the fields. The campers felt awkwardly placed on the raw land, and my father, speaking from experience, remarked that they must flood at least once a year. We drove about halfway down the line of them until we were a good quarter mile from the entrance, and then my father stopped the car and got out. Our car felt very shiny and new in the middle of the big empty field.

My father talked excitedly about how he'd cut down some trees along the river in the middle distance and sawed them up, took them to the mill in Hancock to be cut into lumber, and then came back and built a shed for his new tractor. He pointed toward the place where he thought the shed had probably been situated and then started walking that way, looking around and adjusting his estimate as he went. He was completely absorbed, and he talked faster as new things occurred to him: he'd planted a patch of pumpkins over there; one time his dog had fought a groundhog by those trees; a girlfriend of his had lived in a house over that hill.

I followed along, absorbed in the story, not paying much attention to anything else. But then, a few hundred feet away and over my father's shoulder, I saw a door in one of the trailers open. A man came out, followed by a boy. The man was holding a can and neither of them was dressed for the cold. My dad either didn't see them or ignored them, but when the man and boy got close, I took my glasses off and faced them with a nervous half smile. The man asked if there was anything he could help us with.

My dad turned and looked at the man. He said that he used to farm this land and that he was here to show his son around. It was clear the man was drunk and his eyes were a little swimmy, but he seemed willing to get a satisfactory answer and move on. He nodded, looked at me again and then at my father, and asked if I was his son. It seemed obvious, but my father said yes. The man nodded again, more good-natured now, and said that someone had been breaking into the campers and stealing TVs. He'd lost one just last week and he was just being careful. We agreed and nodded, and there was an awkward silence.

Then, from the corner of my eye, I saw headlights go on in the distance. A big pickup truck rolled through the campground entrance and slowly down the road. It parked behind our car. Even though it was an open field I couldn't help but notice that the driver had effectively blocked us in. Two men got out of the truck, both holding beer cans of their own. Then they came walking toward us, a big man followed by a smaller one. The bigger one had a red face and longish blond hair and was bald on top. He was wearing a T-shirt that said "Army Dad." The smaller man had a long beard and squinted through thick, dirty glasses. He stayed two steps behind.

The big man took a long look at the two of us.

"Did yinz see that sign that said 'Private'?"

"We did see it, yeah, I'm sorry. My dad was just showing—"

"Well if yinz saw it, then why did yinz drive down anyhow?"

I told him that we got confused, and he said that he guessed we did. There was another silence. My father spoke up, friendly, using a tone that refused to acknowledge that there was anything wrong with us being there, and told him that he used to farm this land forty years ago, from right here to about those trees over there.

The man said: "No you didn't."

My father seemed slightly taken aback. He looked around again and then back at the man. He spoke again, in a normal, unexcited way, and said that this was the property line and that he rented the land and farmed it. When the man didn't say anything, my father went on, explaining again that he'd brought his son to see the place and hadn't been back there for almost thirty years. I didn't say anything at all. My father went into the details, that he'd come out here in 1972 and had lived here for three years. He said that he lived up in Huntingdon County now and farmed up there, but he'd gotten his start on this land right here. The man said again: "No you didn't."

My dad started to explain again that he grew crops here, but the man interrupted: "What kind of crops?" He said this in a way that made it seem like he knew that it was marijuana. I looked around to see if there was a wife or a dog or anything else that might be witnessing what was happening. There wasn't. The plastic sheets covering the windows of the nearby trailers snapped in the stiff breeze. My dad said that it was just corn and tomatoes, the usual things, and that he had been pretty young then and had been doing it mostly for fun. The man interrupted again: "You didn't farm here. This land ain't been farmed in forty-six years."

I looked at my father. He was wearing his standard outfit: khakis, a shirt with a collar, and hiking boots. He was holding his bifocals in his hand. He looked like a lawyer out hacking around, or some other professional that didn't belong in a field with trailers and drunk men. The circle of five men started to feel tighter, and I looked again at the others. They were all watching the big blond man, slightly rapt. He was still just putting on a show at this point, a good one, and I was a little transfixed myself. Like the other men, I wanted to know what was going to happen next. My father started to speak again and got most of a sentence out before the man interrupted again: "No you didn't."

There was a moment of long silence, and no one said a word. When my father spoke again, his voice cracked a little. There were similarities in his manner to a man about to cry, a welling up of strong emotion. His eyes took on a damp, glassy look, and he leaned toward the man. Then he pointed at the ground. He said: "Right here. I put tomatoes in the ground right here. I drove my tractor right here. I'll be goddamned if I didn't." The words were released in a slow steady rhythm. This wasn't an argument, it was a recitation of facts. If the man decided to contest those facts, then there was nowhere else to go.

I felt my body tensing against the impossible fact that this blond man might hit my father and that I would be forced to decide what to do about it. Then the man seemed to make a calculation. The tone of his voice changed, like his next question might possibly have an answer.

"Who rented you this land?"

"A German psychiatrist from Washington, DC," my father said.

There was a pause as the man considered this. To me it sounded ridiculous, almost like my father was taunting him with a demonstrably impossible answer.

"Doctor Wien? Hell, he went on back to Germany. I bought this property from him through the mail," the man said. My father pointed at another place on the ground. "This was the line. Tommy Sounders worked the other acres." There was no threat in the statement now; it was as simple as a cartographer pointing out a lesson on a map. The man said, "Aw, Tommy's been dead for some time now. Yinz go ahead and have a look around."

The man took another pull on his beer and headed back to his truck. The little man scurried behind him. My father turned away like nothing had happened and went walking off in the opposite direction, still eager to see if we might find any trace of the shed he had built. We walked to the bank of the river, and my father looked around, surprised that there were trees here, and said he couldn't understand how they got so big. We turned around and looked back over the open field again, but it had been flooded too many times, grown up and mowed down, been planted and picked at by crows, and by now there was nothing left that he could recognize.

The place felt weird to me now, charged somehow. I felt like something momentous had almost happened, something that could have changed both my father and me permanently, and like I'd made a narrow escape. I was eager to get back in the car and go home. But everything still seemed completely normal to my father, and he wasn't in any hurry. He was talking excitedly again, remembering how it had felt to be thirty years old and at the very beginning of the life he led now. I looked around at the old lawn chairs, the car batteries, and the plastic tricycles. As we threaded our way back to the car, a light clicked on in one of the rusty trailers, and a baby started to cry.

4

By the end of June I had been back at the farm for almost a month, and I felt like I needed to get busy doing something that justified leaving Massachusetts, to get started on a task that felt more important than just picking lettuce. For the last few weeks I'd been kicking around a plan in my head, a vague idea about building a place to live so that I wouldn't need to sleep in my old bedroom anymore. Hearing the murmur of my parents' conversation around the kitchen table as I drifted off to sleep felt like I was eavesdropping on their marriage. The idea of building a little cabin wasn't totally out of the blue—I'd been fantasizing about it even when I was still at my desk at the art museum, and eventually I'd daydreamed a simple structure, raised off the ground somehow, and high enough that I'd need a ladder to get on top.

On a Wednesday morning, a day when the farm was quieter

because there was no market to prepare for the next day, I decided to get busy building. I could clearly imagine the structure I wanted to build. It would have space to sit and read out in the open, shaded by the trees and close enough to the creek that I'd be able to hear the water at night. I didn't know the first thing about carpentry, and I'd always been bad at understanding how things were put together in general. I wasn't a tinkerer. I didn't tear things apart to see how they worked. I'd always been bored by Legos. I just had a feeling, though, a certain confidence in my general abilities, that if I really tried, I could make something that would work.

✳

It was early July, always one of the best times of the season, and the mornings were still bright and clear, the ridge cast a long shadow after lunch, and cool air pooled in the hollow in the early evening. The maple trees above the house were still clean and new, without the coat of dust they'd have in August, and my mother's spindly rosebushes were in bloom. The lilacs beside the machine shop buzzed with fat carpenter bees, the green spades of the leaves rustling in the light breeze. It helped the general mood that the farm was running smoothly. There hadn't been any serious disasters yet.

We harvested beets, basil, dill, arugula, parsley, chard, and rhubarb every few days, and three days a week we harvested squash: green zucchini, yellow crooknecks, gold zucchini, and sunburst. The first corn was going to be ready in a week or two, the tomatoes still looked strong and healthy, and the first raspberries would be ripe soon. People joked in the fields and let the truck radio play loudly while they weeded beets or picked beans. There was a general sense of optimism.

It helped that the strawberries were finally over. The crew had been picking them since before I even got home, since the last week of May. The harvest was a horrible job, crawling down the rows on hands and knees for three or fours hours at a stretch, hay sticking to all the sweaty places. They needed to be picked three days a week, and no one ever looked forward to it. The plants were weedy, the berries were hard to find, and the worst part was the nagging feeling that if you went back and looked again you'd find just as many as you had the first time through.

My father was full of praise at the crew meetings. He relaxed and joked, pet the dogs, and went back into the house to finish his breakfast. Although he seemed confident, he almost never went out to the fields. When it was absolutely necessary for him to leave the barnyard, when he had to walk to have a look at a broken piece of equipment or give his opinion of a crop of beets, he would get completely overwhelmed by the details. He saw problems everywhere: with the irrigation, bug damage, the rocks in the newly tilled fields, the spacing of rows, and the weeds in the carrots or the beans.

At this point, my father did most of his work in the barnyard, directing things from there, giving orders and getting reports back. Someone would bring him an ear of corn to evaluate or a bean plant that had been pulled up from the patch, and he would judge the age and condition and suggest a course of action. He was on the phone constantly, or on one of the walkie-talkies, always talking to someone about peas or kale, discussing a new transplanter, arguing with someone about a defective part he'd been sent for one of the tractors. He still worked long days, and he still got his hands greasy, but it was rare that he'd plant a tomato seedling himself, and only then to show someone else how to do it.

The morning that I decided to get started building my cabin was perfect—not too hot—and after I had a cup of coffee I went out the back door, planning to take a long walk all over the farm and scout a location where I could start digging the foundation holes. I looked in all the far corners of the property, a swampy place by the Dogleg, a lonely gully above the Far Field, an exposed spot at the end of the Upper Bottom. I wanted it to feel like a good neighborhood, with mature trees and plenty of sunlight, and I didn't want it to have too many bugs or a view of an irrigation pump.

After a few hours of tramping around I came back to the house and had lunch, then helped my mother seed cauliflower in the greenhouse for a few hours. Then, in the late afternoon, once it was cooler and the buzz of the cicadas had dropped down from its high whine, I went out to look again. This time I walked out across the open fields behind the barn, over the three gentle humps of the fields there, following the track of the road that ran across them. I came to the edge of the last field, where the land fell away in a steep slope. I was a half mile from the barnyard, and I could still see the side of the barn lit up by the sun, but I was too far away to be picked out in the high grass.

An old beehive sat at the edge of the slope, wrapped in chicken wire to keep the bears away, and it buzzed in the warm afternoon. I could see one of the apprentice's shacks, maybe a quarter mile away and built against a line of trees, but it was on the opposite side of a wide gulf of empty meadow. Below me, down the slope and hidden away, the grass on the hillside was high and green, and a grove of young black walnut trees made a dappled shade. A faint path, maybe worn by deer, led over the edge of the hill. A bramble of wild blackberries looked shady and cool. It felt like a secret spot.

The patch of ground wasn't on the way to any place else, and the slope of the hill meant that nobody would bother to come down there for any practical reason. It had a long view of the Dogleg, and the field directly below me was planted in cabbages. I could see the rows of them through a break in the trees, thousands of green globes laid out in neat, curving lines. Beyond the field there were tall tulip trees that ran along the creek bank. The ridge rose steeply on the opposite bank, and I could see the glint of a car as it made its way along the dirt road that ran along the top, far above me.

There were places like this on the farm, spots very close to the roads and the fields that nobody ever really thought about, not concealed exactly but blank. I'd forgotten about this space myself and hadn't considered it until I saw that little path meandering into the grass. A hunter might walk through this grove of walnut trees sometimes—looking for deer and rabbits in their hiding places—but it was useless for anything to do with the work of the farm. It was partly that feeling that made it so attractive, surrounded by the fields but also separate.

I realized that one of the only people who had used this part of the farm before was Bert. In the early 1980s, before Bert moved away from Washington, my father had hired him and a man named Jeff to build a cabin in this same location. The structure had a woodstove so that it could be used later in the season, as well as a porch that was the perfect place to sit after work and watch the twilight descend. The grass in that spot was so green and the trees were so well spaced because the cabin had burned down on a winter night a few years later. It was too remote for fire trucks to get there, and the building was built entirely of dry wood, and when it was done, just the nails glowed hot red in the ashes. The space where I was standing now was a kind of scar that it left.

I remembered hanging out with Bert as he'd helped build it. He'd showed me how to toenail a stud and let me play with the chalk line marker, pulling the string back and letting it snap, and he had showed me how the spirit level worked. It wasn't the only structure he'd built on our farm— the summer kitchen was also his work, as were two of the original cabins that the apprentices lived in—but they'd picked this spot specifically because it was the nicest one on the farm, and because an old giant walnut tree—the same tree that still stood there now—would shade the cabin and keep it cool.

☀

Once I decided on the spot I went back to the house and sat on the back porch to talk with my mother while she weeded sage in the garden below. I was excited and eager to get started, and I told her how I'd begin with the basics, building the foundation and floor first, which would give me a platform

out in the woods where I could pitch a tent. Then, after I'd
slept there for a few weeks, felt out the location, and made
sure that the structure was sturdy enough, I'd consider a roof
and four walls. She didn't stop weeding, but she listened to
everything I said. I gave her credit that she didn't question
whether it was a good idea.

After dinner I went back out to the barnyard and looked at
the other buildings to see if I could get some clues about how
to proceed. Most of them were simple structures, with exposed
joints and straightforward dimensions, easy enough to reproduce. I went behind the barn and looked at the structure that
supported a propane tank. It was built into a steep slope, and it
was strong enough to hold the huge metal egg of that steel
container, which was way more weight than I ever expected to
put on my own floor. I noted how big the pilings were and how
the joists were spaced and how they were all connected.

Afterward I went through the desk in my old bedroom,
found a sheet of graph paper, and sat at the kitchen table to
sketch out a simple plan. I drew a rectangle for the top of the
platform and a triangle to indicate how it would sit on the
slope. I counted out the squares on the paper and made each
one equal to one foot so that I wouldn't get confused. I spaced
the joists and pilings based on the platform I'd just looked at,
and I erred on the side of caution so that it could bear more
weight than it needed to. Then I used the Pythagorean theo-
rem to calculate various lengths of the platform, erased the
stray pencil marks, and made neat figures along each line.

I'd sketched something that looked a lot like a dock on a
lake. The back of the structure was anchored on the ground,

where the shoreline would have been, and when the slope fell away, beneath it, there was an empty space instead of deep water. The overall effect would be a platform suspended way up high, cantilevered in midair among the branches of the walnut trees. Even with the drama of the sketch, and the way it made the structure seem precarious and delicate, I still wasn't worried. I could trace how everything tied together, feel how it would connect to the ground and the simple way that the deck would sit on top.

My father came in while I was sketching and went to wash his hands. The water was scalding, and the steam rose up around him while he scrubbed. I explained what I wanted to do. He looked at my drawings, said, "Hmmm, sounds OK," and went back to scrubbing. I knew he was distracted by a problem with a delivery of chicken feed, but I still felt I needed him to sign off on it.

"Do you think it'll work?"

"Let me see," he said, and took the sheet of paper. He studied it for a moment. "Sure. Why not."

That was all I wanted; now he couldn't be surprised if it ended up being a disaster.

✳

The next step was digging holes for the foundation posts. It was a less exciting job than the planning, but it still felt good to get started. I found a measuring tape, a post-hole digger and digging bar, and gathered up little white flags to mark out the perimeter of the site. I commandeered one of the pickups, threw everything in the back, and drove out to the edge of the slope. I stood in the same spot I had the day before and planted my first flag, and then I used the measuring tape to figure out where the others should be. I marked six different spots, forming the shape of a long rectangle, and then I started digging the holes for the first set of posts.

The posts had to be installed thirty-six inches deep so that they wouldn't be affected by the frost heaves when the ground froze, but the soil was full of shale, and the digging was harder than I'd anticipated. I used the heavy digging bar to chip and smash away at the shale and then I used the post-hole digger to pull it out. The hole was narrow and deep, so taking the dirt out was like emptying a beer bottle of sand using a long pair of tweezers. I smashed for a while and then dug, smashed and dug.

The sun had come up, and it was getting hot. Once the hole was too deep for the digger, I had to reach in and pull the loose dirt out by hand. I lay there on the grass, my arms sunk into the ground up to my shoulder, and pulled out the rock handful by handful. The sweat dripped off my face and made mud, my T-shirt turned deep brown at the sleeve, and when I scratched the inside of my ear with my pinkie I pulled it out covered in grit. After three hours of work I finally figured the first hole was deep enough. I sat in the grass and listened to the sounds that the flags made as the slips of white plastic flapped on the ends of their wires.

✳

At lunchtime I went back up to the house. My mother was at the dining room table counting money from the Saturday market, making neat stacks of ones, fives, tens, and twenties, and a separate stack of checks. It was a lot of money, all of it in small bills, and it was hard to resist the urge to play with it. I grabbed a handful, but she slapped my hand away. She hummed while she worked, and I moved some of the cash aside to set down my ham sandwich.

After forty years in business, my parents still made their living by going to market in Washington three days a week, a small market on Tuesday afternoons, a big one on Saturday mornings, and then another on Sunday. The Sunday market was organized by a group of farmers, but the other two were just our farm, and they were set up in a school yard in Cleveland Park, a neighborhood of rambling old houses and mature trees.

"So, how's it going down there?" she asked.

"I dug a hole."

"Your dad was looking for you. They're getting squash at two, and they need another person for the crew."

"I'm not picking squash today," I said.

"I wouldn't either. It's hot as hell," she said, then got up. "If anyone is looking for me tell them that I took all the barn cats to the vet to get wormed."

She finished her cereal, put her boots on, and went out to catch as many kittens as she could manage while I sat there at the table thinking about the lumber I'd need for my plans. I went out and found my father at his desk in his office. The stacks of paper around him had accumulated over decades: seed catalogues, planting schedules, file folders bursting with old handwritten financial statements. The barrel of his rifle stuck out from under a drift of equipment manuals. Post-it notes were pressed to everything with scrawls on them that said "call chicken feed" and "check the temp" and "cider on Tuesday."

He was shuffling everything around and talking to someone on the phone about asparagus when I walked in. I stood there quietly and looked at the forty years of mementos tacked up on the walls: a poem someone had written for him about blueberry pie; a picture of him, thirty-five years old, standing in the snow in Washington selling apples to people in polyester leisure suits; a postcard of Ronald Reagan with a Hitler mustache drawn on it; a picture I'd drawn when I was four, of a superhero with a lollipop; an award from the governor of Pennsylvania; a papier-mâché turnip; an Emerson quote that my little sister had written out in Magic Marker about "the suggestion of an occult relation between man and the vegetable."

He got off the phone, and I asked him where he thought I should get lumber.

"Why, are you building something?"

I reminded him about what I was doing out above the Dogleg.

"Oh yeah, yeah, right. Sorry." Then he sat and stared out the window.

"Hmmmm," he said.

"Do you think it's a bad idea?" I asked.

"What? Oh, no. It sounds great. Sorry, I'm thinking about that asparagus. No, I think it sounds great."

I asked him if he wanted to come down and see it, but he said he was too busy, and I was secretly relieved.

"Do you remember who that guy is with the sawmill in Hares Valley?" I asked. He picked up an old notebook and flipped through it.

"It's here somewhere. Zinoble I think it is."

He looked some more.

"Ah shit, I don't know. Zinoble. Look him up."

The phone rang again, and he picked it up.

"Jim Crawford. No, we don't have any more chickens."

He raised his eyebrows to ask if there was anything else I needed from him right then. I whispered thanks and left.

✵

I didn't know if it was the one I was looking for, but I called the first Zinoble in the phone book. A woman picked up.

"Morning," I said. "I was looking for some lumber."

"This is Bobby's. You want his brother Mike," she said.

"Do you know where I can reach him?"

"Hold on a second." I heard the spring on a screen door stretch and the frame hit the wall. She yelled.

"Bobby! Where's Mike at? Someone on the phone wants wood."

She came back on the phone.

"Go over to his place near around four. He should be up there. You know where it's at?"

I didn't.

"We're up in Hares Valley. Go over the second bridge after the Methodist church and look for the saw blade nailed up on the right. Take that road back and you can't miss it."

Before I left the house I added up the basic amounts of

wood that I needed. I could have just taken my plans and shown the guy what I had in mind, but I didn't want to look like an amateur. Even as it stood now, I was afraid he might ask what I was building, and I didn't know exactly how to explain it. I decided that if he asked I would just tell him I was building a shed.

I drove over in the black Ford, and on the third pass I spotted a rusty circular-saw blade nailed to a tree. From there I followed an electric line that had been propped up on notched sticks high enough so that logging trucks could get under it. After a mile or so of ruts and puddles, the thick woods suddenly stopped, and the ground was bare as far as I could see. In the distance an old dump truck from the fifties was parked with the entire front half of the vehicle submerged in mud. The motor had been hooked, via a series of open belts and gears, to the machine that ran the saw, and smoke was belching from the whole crazy operation.

I drove up and stopped my truck outside the shed. There were four men working there, huddled around a huge open blade, wrestling logs up and pushing them into the teeth, and stacking the planks that fell off to one side. Occasionally there was an ugly sound and a spray of sparks would fly out, but no one stopped working. Everyone ignored me, but I was too nervous to get any closer to the blade, so I just stood there watching. Eventually I cupped my hands around my mouth and yelled to them. They looked up, and I realized that they hadn't known I was there. One of them left his place and came walking toward me.

He was wearing an apron made of thick, creased hide, and

in the front pockets there were wicked-looking pincers and knives with oddly shaped blades. I told him what I was looking for, and he pointed toward some stacks in the distance. My worries about explaining myself suddenly seemed stupid; he couldn't care less what I was building. "Them over there we just cut, but the ones to the right are ready. Holler when you're done." I pulled the truck up to one of the piles and started loading the lumber. The weight of it made the bed sag on its springs, and the sap bled off the yellow boards.

When I was done I went back over to the shed where the men were now sitting and smoking, taking a break. The blade had stopped, and one of them was pounding on something with a short sledgehammer.

"That Jim Crawford's boy?" one of them called out to me.

"That's me."

"How yinz doin' this season?"

"All right, all right. Can't complain I guess. Not really liking this heat."

"Did you just move back?"

"Just home to visit."

"Where were you living before then?"

"Massachusetts."

"No shit! Massachusetts! What were you getting up to there?"

"I worked at an art museum."

"An art museum!"

"Yeah."

I decided not to elaborate on this, and there was a long pause while the guy in charge took the money that I'd counted out and made change out of the greasy bills in his apron pocket.

"Long way from Massachusetts, eh? You going to take the home place over?"

"I don't plan on it. Too much work for me."

"Damn straight. Well, that's a nice piece of land you have up there, a real nice farm. Tell him I said hello."

I thanked him, got in the truck, and drove back out the road.

On the way home I stopped at the hardware store to buy nails. The lumberyard had been pretty easy because there wasn't much to choose from, but the nails were more difficult. I didn't understand the measuring system, which used "pennies," a unit that had nothing to do with how much they cost, and the abbreviation for penny was "d," but due to differences in finish, one "8d" nail wasn't necessarily the same as other "8d" nails. I looked at various sizes, held them in my hand until I found a size that seemed trustworthy, and bought a few pounds.

*

Three days later, after various interruptions and setbacks, I'd dug all six of the foundation holes. It was late afternoon by then. I felt wrung out and completely bored by the digging. I leaned the shovel against a walnut tree and sat down to pick at my blisters. There was no way to get electric power so far away from the barnyard, so all the work had to be done by hand. I appreciated that it was going to feel good to work this way but I also dreaded it. I sat there and looked at my three days of hard labor. There were six small mounds of dirt beside six deep holes. They looked like tiny graves.

I'd carried the lumber down earlier in the day, struggling with the dead weight of the long six by fours, wrangling them down the slope one by one. When I dropped one, it tumbled away from me and crushed all the flowers and small saplings in its path. When it finally stopped, all tangled up and propped at an awkward angle in a damp spot at the bottom of the hill, I went down to retrieve it, dragging a muddy rut behind me. Eventually all the wood was stacked neatly like enormous gold matchsticks.

After a few more minutes' rest, I picked up the long posts and tipped each of them into the holes. Suddenly, where there had just been grass and flowers, there were long posts shooting out of the ground in all different directions. They looked random and out of context and nothing like what I'd had in my head. A sparrow swooped in and perched on the tip of one of them. It looked around nervously for a second, then flew off.

That night I brought up the building with my father again.

"I've got the holes dug down there."

"What?" he said. "Holes?"

"Yeah, for the thing I'm building."

"Oh. Jesus, Arlo, I'm sorry. Show me again."

I went and got my sketch.

"Did you get everything below the frost line?"

I told him that I had. He held the sheet of graph paper and followed everything. It wasn't very complicated, and it didn't take him very long.

"Did you already sink the posts?"

"Yeah."

He looked harder.

"Really?" he said. "It take you a long time?"

"Yeah," I said.

"Is it true?"

*

It wasn't true. In fact the idea of something being "true"—the most basic rule in building, which calls for everything to be square and equal, and the kind of geometric problem that I'd never been able to really grasp—was totally new to me. What it meant in practice was that if any one angle was off, even one that seemed small and insignificant, it could compound through the rest of the structure, growing bigger as it went. The basic integrity of the building depended on it; a mistake in the foundation could make the roof leak or, worse, just cause the whole thing to fall over in the middle of the night. My father explained all this to me and how important it was, and then he patted me on the back.

After dinner I went back down and looked at the posts again. I wasn't just slightly off; instead of a rectangle with ninety-degree angles I'd dug something closer to a parallelogram. It was a basic mistake, but I felt stupid. In my rush to get going I'd assumed that I knew what I was doing, and I hadn't asked for any help. Now I'd wasted days of digging holes that were completely useless. I cursed and kicked one of the posts and threw the shovel out into the grass. Then I yanked the posts out of the ground and filled the holes back in, which took no more than ten minutes total.

Finding these kinds of mistakes was my father's specialty. His entire business, for forty years, had been based on tempering his enthusiasms with an obsessive attention to detail. He looked over a freshly plowed field and saw where the drainage would be bad, examined a truckload of ripe peaches and picked out the first ones to rot, looked at a new puppy and saw the dead chickens it would eventually drag into the yard.

That night I sat with my father at the kitchen table with four pencils and a long piece of thread. He showed me how to square the angles and how to make the structure sound, and in the morning I took a piece of rope and did the same thing with the posts, measuring out equal lengths so that I had a rectangle with right angles. I spent another day and a half digging new holes, and then I put the posts back in them. I sat down again and looked at my work. It looked better. From now on I'd look for mistakes every step of the way.

*

I knew that I wasn't the first guy to think that building a cabin in the woods was a great idea. I wasn't even the first person to build a cabin on this particular hillside. In general the impulse was pretty common on the farm. An apprentice had built a tree house along the creek when I was thirteen, a wildly ambitious building with one room and a skylight, a bunk, and a trapdoor. It had seven windows of all different dimensions, some six feet high, some tiny and angular, and one that had a view that looked up directly into the crown of the tree.

I went down to check it out the next day and stood in the

cool air off the creek, the dark-green umbrellas of the may-apple plants rustling around my feet. The structure was still up there in the branches, slightly lopsided but with the same sense of proportions and careful lines that it had been built with. I climbed up and wedged myself into the crotch of the tree. There was enough room to sit comfortably, and I looked down and admired the view of the creek, then I scrambled up through the trapdoor and went into the room above me.

The builder had been an architecture student at Yale before he started farming, and the building was a technical marvel. It sat easily in the embrace of the tree, and the interior felt like a tightly fitted jewel box. There was a ladder that led up to a hatch in the ceiling and from there to a tiny crow's nest, a perch that served no purpose except for extreme vertigo. He'd also managed to suspend a deck off the side of the building by hanging it from steel cables and connecting it to the rest of the building by a floating staircase. Then he covered it with Astroturf and made a putting green by cutting a hole in the far corner.

I walked out onto the deck and felt the slight give of the floor as it flexed against the anchor of the steel cables. There were no railings, and I noted how the floor just dropped off into space, a feeling that I realized I wanted to replicate in my own structure. I stood there and thought for a second of the guy who'd built it, how he might line up his putt on the new green while pushing his long blond hair behind his ears. I stepped carefully over to a round hole at the edge. There were four golf balls still in there, one red, one yellow, one green, and one blue.

✳

The next day, after I'd fixed the spacing of the pilings on my own structure, replaced the posts and made them steady, I got started on hanging the floor. By now I felt more confident than I had at any point in the process, and I was starting to enjoy how the structure balanced against itself, how it was all one piece. I made small adjustments with the handsaw, took out nails and replaced them, found the places where boards weren't perfectly flush and fit them back together more precisely. The structure was coming together as a tight box, a rectangle with obvious shape and symmetry.

In the afternoon I went around to the top and started to lay the floorboards across that box, starting from the back and moving out as I went. The floor felt sturdy under my feet. Now that I was in the homestretch I got a little giddy, singing out loud and beating the nails in harder than I needed to. I lay down the last board, squared it, nailed it down, and I could feel the slight tug of momentum as I hammered. I tried not to look over the edge and see the long drop. When I was done I hung the hammer on the edge of the platform from its claw foot, lay spread-eagle on the floor, and looked up into the branches.

I listened to the soft roar of an irrigation pump in the far distance, the small sounds of the rabbits and the birds in the blackberry bramble, the tiny creaks and pops of the structure as the weight adjusted. I got up and walked off into the grass a short distance so that I could see the whole thing at once. The thin line of the floor was held up high on its delicate legs,

a clean plane in the green leaves. It was articulated and graceful, and it was strange looking. It looked exactly like what I'd
pictured in my mind when I'd first set out.

⚹

I was exhausted at dinner and went to bed early. In the morning I returned to the platform to make some small adjustments
and to clean up the empty boxes of nails and collect the hammers, saws, and measuring tapes strewn around in the high
grass. Once everything looked perfect, I went to find my
father. We walked down through the fields, and he stopped
to look at a shoddy cultivation job.

"Do you see any deer in the evenings down here? I swear,
I let those hunters come and they just sit down here and drink
beer and don't shoot the damn things."

"I haven't seen any."

He squinted along the sight line for any sign of them.

"Have there been hunters down here the last few days?" I
asked.

"Yeah, a guy came down from Cassville yesterday."

I remembered hearing a shot in the afternoon and dismiss-
ing it, but now I realized that no one knew I was out in the
woods and wouldn't expect there to be someone on that slope.

"Can you tell me when the next guy comes, please?"

My father looked at me like I was being ridiculous.

"I knew you were down here," he said. "I told him to be
careful."

We stopped to look at some rhubarb roots that had been
dug up for replanting, tuberous masses that looked like cow

hearts, still wet where they'd been cut open by the shovel. He was complaining that they hadn't finished the job, but when he came over the edge of the hill and saw the platform, he stopped talking all at once. He walked down to the structure slowly, taking it in, and walked underneath and ran his hands over the long joists, and then kicked the bottom of the pilings, turning his foot so that he could hit them with the full force of his boot sole. He reached up to a piece of bracing and yanked on it, trying to pull out the nails. Then he went around to the front, leaned his full weight against one of the pilings, and shoved as hard as he could. He looked kind of silly, like a character in an old slapstick movie trying to push over a house. "Well, it's true," he said.

It was quiet for a minute or two as we both contemplated the thing from the ground. Then he went up to the top, stepped out on the floor, and walked briskly to the very edge. My responsibility for his safety suddenly welled up in me. I considered asking him to stop, telling him that I wasn't sure if he should go so far out, but by then he was high above the ground, craning his neck to look down over the drop. Then, like a little kid having a tantrum, he bunched up his fists, crouched down, and jumped up as high as he could, landing heavily on both feet. He did it three or four more times and then stopped. The structure barely budged. When he turned around, he was beaming. I beamed back.

✶

That afternoon I went out and pitched a tent on the floor. It wasn't that I was giving up on the idea of building something

more complicated, but I liked the structure so much the way
that it was, and it had taken so much work to build it, that I
thought I might just sleep in the tent for a while and see how
it worked out. Sarah would be coming in another week; the
two-man tent would be tight, but we could fit.

That night after dinner I walked out along the road so I
could spend my first night there. The moon was near full, and
the air was thick and soft; the hollow felt like it was filled with
a deep warm ocean. Fireflies clung to the dark trees and drifted
in the open space, their phosphorescence riding the slow cur-
rents. I got to the edge of the hill and saw the silvery plane of
the platform hovering there among the trees on the hillside
below me. I'd brought some pillows and books and a jar of
cold water, and I'd also hung a flashlight inside from the peak
of the roof and now it made the curves and angles of the tent
glow with a weird green light.

I went down through the black weeds and stood on what
I'd built. I could honestly say that the platform was the most
beautiful object I'd ever made in my entire life. I'd also
brought a bottle of Wild Turkey down with me, and I took it
out to the far edge and sat down with my feet dangling in the
dark. I lay back and watched the stars through the branches
of the walnut trees, and eventually I crawled into the tent and
went to sleep.

5

A week later it was time for me to go pick up Sarah from the airport. This would be her second visit to the farm; the first was at Christmas the winter before. We'd only been dating for a few months at that point, but she'd been game for everything. She pulled on rubber boots to collect eggs, helped my mother plant arugula in the greenhouse, went for long walks through the bare woods. There'd been deep snow in the days before we arrived, and the implements out in the fields were all plushly upholstered with it, the long lines of the landscape muted and soft, the creek running along the bottom of the ridge, black and quick under glassy ice.

We walked in the silent fields enjoying the feeling of arctic loneliness, and when we trekked out across the open spaces, we left a wandering dotted line of footsteps across the hills. At some point we came across five raised lines of snow run-

ning down the field, and I dug down until I found an unhar-
vested cabbage, icy and frozen bright green. The long drone
of a plane went over, and I instinctively waved, somehow thinking that they would pick out the two bright spots of our jackets in all the frozen white.

Sarah's willingness and enthusiasm had been encouraging
then and had made me think that she might take to the place.
Now it was July though, and everything was squirming and
alive, and everywhere there was a low rumble of pickups and
tractors, a crackle of radios and intercoms, a mumble of half-
heard conversations about vegetables. Even the dogs seemed
busy, escorting the trucks out of the barnyard, providing lax
supervision to the crews moving slowly down the rows, lazily
patrolling the edges of the fields, and only occasionally wandering off to find a dead animal in the woods or to drink from
a mud puddle.

Sarah and I had been talking every few days on the
phone, conversations that echoed on her end in the empti-
ness of our old apartment, and I'd tried, in the ways that I
could, to give her a sense of how the farm worked. Most days
in July looked similar to this: First, before the heat of midday,
there would be a harvest of chard and cilantro and parsley,
and then the crew would split up, and some would go to pick
green beans while another collected knives to do the squash
harvest. The same crew would move to cucumbers while others transplanted corn, then basil, and, if it didn't get dark first,
kale. In the greenhouse someone would spend the whole day
planting broccoli and collards.

The planting and harvesting was only part of it. There

was also all the infrastructure to be maintained—the irrigation pumps, the Japanese beetle traps in the raspberries, the galvanized steel feeders for the chickens. The electrician would come to look at a problem with the cooler, and someone would help him take apart the compressor and check the lines. Manure would be spread in the End Patch. All the roads would be mowed with the Bush Hog and the compost bins rotated.

And if it was a Friday, a Saturday, or a Monday we'd prepare for the market the next day. The cooler had to be organized, the hundreds of boxes stacked onto pallets four feet deep by four feet wide by eight feet high, ready to be rolled off the loading docks the next morning. The display tables would be washed, the price signs written, and the shopping baskets organized. Someone would replace the batteries in the scales, fill the calculators with paper for receipts, and fill the cash boxes with change.

And it would only get busier in the next few weeks. Once the corn started, there would be early-morning harvests at six thirty, and soon the green beans and snap peas would require a permanent crew of pickers. The basil plants were thriving in the heat, the squash harvests were getting heavier, and there was a surprising amount of rhubarb. The tomatoes were on the horizon; the first generation already had green fruit, the second was flowering, and the third and fourth generations were big enough to be staked.

As healthy as the plants looked, though, the tomato blight, relegated to a watchful waiting state in the prior weeks, was now a more serious concern. A farmer in Mifflin County, a man involved in the co-op and a friend of my father, had found it in his crop a week before, and there were reports coming in from big commercial growers all along the East Coast. The affected farms were all at least fifty miles from ours, and those infections didn't pose any immediate threat, but they were still an occasion to worry. If it stayed dry, and the spores didn't have the water they needed to reproduce and spread, then it was much more likely that it wouldn't infect our own crop.

We were still taking some precautions. People working in the tomatoes were being careful not to move from one patch to another without changing any clothes that had come in contact with the plants. Tobacco could carry some diseases, so everyone washed their hands carefully after smoking. Even though the farm was organic and didn't have access to traditional fungicides, there were some approved treatments, including a solution of copper sprayed on the foliage. The tomato manager did this a few times a week, hoping that it would kill the spores, and eventually his work boots turned as green as an old penny.

The topic of the blight was coming up often at the morning meetings, but my father wasn't panicking. He was familiar with the danger from his first season when the blight had taken the whole crop, and from a few others when particularly wet weather had allowed it to thrive in isolated patches. He knew how much damage it could do, but for now he wasn't showing much outward concern.

✳

I wasn't sure how I felt about Sarah joining me at the farm for these highest, busiest months of the season. On one hand I couldn't wait to see her, but on the other I'd adapted quickly to being home again. I liked the strangeness of living on my platform in the trees, always being dirty, never seeing strangers, walking home alone at night through the fields. Part of me was afraid that Sarah might break that spell, but more than that, I worried that none of it would impress her, that she'd get bored or unhappy, and that she'd want to leave.

My plan was for the both of us to sleep in the tent together and both work on the farm and eat our meals with my parents. Sarah could join the crew of apprentices for five or six hours a day and also help my mother in the greenhouse, the herb garden, with cutting cheese for market and counting money. But even if she didn't mind that work, or even if she took to it, I knew that we were still going to be out there together in the middle of nowhere for three long months.

Obviously Sarah was going to need some time to get used to things, and it was generally understood that she wasn't there to work too hard. She was looking more for a break in her normal routine, and her summer was supposed to be about doing the unexpected, maybe learning a little more about vegetables and spending some time outside. Even if I secretly hoped that she'd fall in love with the place, I wasn't going to push it on her.

Regardless though, whether this was a vacation or something more serious, she was completely committed to it. Once she left Massachusetts there wasn't any place for either of us to go back to; Sarah had given notice at her job, had wound down her projects, and cashed in her 401 K. We'd sold all our furniture on the Internet and found someone to take over our lease. She'd locked the door of our apartment for the last time, dropped the key in the mailbox, and now, for the foreseeable future, we officially lived in a tent at the back of my parents' farm.

✳

On the morning that Sarah was due to arrive I'd been sleeping in the tent for a week, and the space was already overly familiar. When I woke up in the morning the close air smelled like my sleep, my dirty body, and the farm. The sheets were dusty and full of sticks and dry grass. I kept my boots inside, and they made the air smell like leather. Sometimes a dog followed me back in the night, and I, happy for the company, let her sleep inside. Now, with the sun seeping through the nylon and making the light a sickly green, I wished I hadn't.

It was two weeks into July now and near the beginning of my second month at the farm, and my morning routine at the tent already felt completely normal. I went outside into the cold morning, shivering, naked, and got dressed under the overhanging trees, dripping with dew from the leaves. Small vines were making their first tentative attempts to engage with the new structure in their midst, climbing the trunks of the surrounding walnut trees and creeping their tiny feelers into the gaps in the lumber. The air was misty, the calls of the crows died in the thick air, and the sun was already a flat gray disc in the sky.

I cleaned up the tent, folded my dirty clothes, collected glasses that were half-full with rain, and stashed the whiskey bottle in the grass so that it wasn't the first thing that Sarah would see. I'd done some things over the past week to make the place feel more homey: hung hooks for my shirt and pants from one of the joists underneath the floor and collected a small library of books that had already gone wavy in the damp. I'd also made a sitting area out at the very edge of the plat-form, with two red canvas chairs and a little table, and a lan-tern suspended from a branch above so that it threw a neat circle of light over everything. I thought that it looked cozy, and I hoped Sarah would feel the same.

I worked for three hours before I left for the airport; I har-vested chard, spent an hour or two picking beans, and then went down to the barnyard and washed up. I rinsed the dust off my neck, combed my hair with my fingers, and thought about going inside to brush my teeth but just decided to eat an apple instead. My dirty jeans looked a little more pre-sentable after I'd beat some of the dust out of them with my hands, and my baseball cap didn't smell quite as bad once I'd rinsed the stale sweat out of it. I checked my teeth in the side mirror of one of the pickups.

As I was pulling out of the barnyard I heard my father's office door slam behind me. I considered just driving on so that he wouldn't have a chance to weigh me down with a bunch of errands, but I stopped. He rarely left the farm at the height of the summer, sometimes not even driving past the mailbox at the bottom of the hill for two or three weeks at a time. This was an opportunity for him to hand over a list of all the things that he needed from outside and that he couldn't get the UPS guy to drop off.

My father had always spent a huge amount of time in his office, at least twelve or fourteen hours a day. He took long breaks for meals, but he was almost always at his desk until late at night. He mostly talked on the phone or met with the different people who knocked quietly and came to sit in the old kitchen chair beside his desk. His phone calls were to all kinds of people: the mechanic who was changing the tires on the truck, the woman who ran the orchard where he bought plums, a customer who wanted to place a special order for a flat of blueberries to be picked up at market on Saturday. His meetings were usually with the crew leader and the field manager, but he also talked to each of the other apprentices regularly. He spent hours talking with the part-time accountant and with the woman in charge of organizing the packing shed. He also met with other farmers who might have been dropping off produce down at the co-op, or with a carpenter who was expanding the tractor shed to accommodate a new piece of equipment.

He also did paperwork, sorting through the enormous pile of bills and invoices he kept in the lid of a tomato box, filling out tax forms, and signing checks. He didn't have a computer, relying on the accountant to do most of the work that required one, and he wrote everything by hand. He went out into the barnyard to check the delivery of a roll of chicken wire or a new wheelbarrow, and he went to the fields when he was absolutely needed, but he also spent a great deal of time inside. He kept a pair of binoculars on his desk so that he could look out his window and see the thermometer down by the greenhouse, and he called an apprentice on the radio if he saw that it was overheating.

"Are you going out?" My father stood there staring at something down in the field, distracted.

"I'm going to the airport to pick up Sarah. I'm already an hour late," I said.

He handed me a crumpled piece of paper on which he had scribbled various tasks.

"OK, I need you to do this list."

Among other things, all written in the handwriting of an emergency room doctor, it said: "pk up manure, get bb at menn (j. peachy), 8 scrn drs."

"I can't do all this," I said. "Plus I'm not showing up with a truck full of manure when I pick up Sarah."

"You can pick the manure up on the way home, after you get her. Just take one of the pickups."

I considered driving into the arrivals section of Dulles Airport in the red Chevy, slightly wobbly on its bent frame, the cab full of knives, and the plastic milk jug of extra gas stashed under the seat for emergencies.

"I'm not picking her up in the red Chevy. Plus it's leaking gas everywhere."

"Hmmm," he said, making it clear that I was being entirely unreasonable.

I ignored him and moved on to the next item on the list.

"They aren't going to have eight screen doors at the True Value."

"They might. Seems like you could at least ask."

"No. I'll get the blueberries. That's it."

"Fine," he said, catching sight of the dust rising up at the bottom of the hill, the signal that a truck was coming up from the bottom. "Just get the blueberries. That Mennonite in . . ." He broke off and cupped his hands around his mouth to yell toward the crew, "Hey, HEY. How many beans did you guys get? I said, HOW MANY . . . Oh, never mind."

Then he ran off.

✳

The airport seemed much bigger than I remembered it, the acres of concrete more blinding, and the complicated approaches more confusing. The crowds surged out of the doors of the terminal, and I stopped carefully as the cross-walks flooded with them. The car I was driving was covered in dust, and it stood out clearly in the stream of shiny SUVs flowing in from the suburbs of Maryland and northern Virginia. I felt like a hick, and I didn't want to walk around in the cool, clean airport in my boots and torn jeans.

Suddenly I saw Sarah waving frantically at me from the curb. I parked, stepped out into the heat of the afternoon, kissed her for a long minute while a policeman moved toward us, already shooing us along. I loaded her bags, opened the passenger side door, and went around and got back behind the wheel. I ignored the honking while we had another kiss. She smelled like her soap and shampoo, and like our old apartment. She pulled away, brushed the hair out of her face, set down her paperback, and appraised me.

"Look at you!" she said. I hoped that I still looked a little bit like a cowboy, but I was starting to suspect that I just looked like a slob.

"You like it?" I asked.

"You smell like cigarettes," she said, and wrinkled her nose.

"Yeah, I guess I like it."

Then she sat back and looked me over again.

"When was the last time you took a shower?"

I had to think about it for a second or two.

"Tuesday."

She looked at me more closely, found a spot on my face that seemed acceptably clean, and gave me another quick peck.

"Well, you kind of smell," she said. "Let's get out of here."

I had almost forgotten what she looked like. She seemed so cool and collected that it made me feel clumsy in comparison. Her sunglasses perched atop her smooth dark hair, her light jacket draped around her narrow frame, and her bag lay neatly in her lap. She was a good traveler, well prepared and self-contained, and I was a rube, worried about getting lost and nervous around the pedestrians. Sarah went through her bag and found chapstick, applied it to the sharp line of her lips, looked in the mirror, and picked an eyelash from her cheek.

We left the airport and headed west, into the horse country of Virginia and over the Potomac, past Antietam, where the bloodiest battle of the Civil War was marked with stone cairns. Sarah looked out the window as we went along, watching the view and filling me in about what had been happening back

in Massachusetts, occasionally stopping to point out some
pretty barn or to ask a question about some crop or livestock.
I was positive and enthusiastic, and I tried not to sound like I
was selling it too hard. When we came into Pennsylvania I
pointed out the low line of the ridges in the distance and the
general direction of the farm.

Before we got home we still had to pick up the blueberries. Even though I'd been annoyed when my father had asked
me to do the errand, I was happy for the scenic detour. I turned
at the Twin Kiss ice cream bar and paused at the one-lane
bridge so that an old man in a black pickup could go first. I
pointed out the mailbox with Peachy, the Mennonite's name,
welded neatly on the side, and we drove up the straight lane
toward the square house. Out in the distance there were three
men working around an implement in the windrows of hay,
but otherwise all was quiet. I pulled up and parked under the
overhang of the barn.

I figured that this would be a good way to reintroduce Sarah
to Pennsylvania and something she definitely wouldn't do
back in Massachusetts. The Mennonites, with their orderly
fields and bonnets, were undeniably charming. The barnyard was swept and empty, with a white barn on a cinder-
block foundation, four chickens pecking under the shade of
a walnut tree, and a plain stone house with a line of black
rubber boots on the back porch. We could see for long distances in every direction, out toward the fields of green
corn gone slightly hazy in the sun. The land on this side of
the ridges was open and flat, with older churches and farmhouses that felt established and permanent. We listened to

the gentle flap of the long dresses hung on a clothesline in the backyard.

I knew that the women inside the house would attend to us when they were done with whatever they were doing, so we just sat in the car and waited for them. Sarah opened the copy of *Anna Karenina* that she'd been reading on the plane, then set it down again, folded her hands in her lap, and closed her eyes. Eventually the back door opened and a girl with two long braids came out; she was maybe ten years old and was wearing a plain dress and an apron. A small dog ran out from the barn and jumped and yapped at her, but she ignored it and shaded her eyes to see who was waiting. She was as cute as a button, and I elbowed Sarah so that she could have a look.

I wanted to seem like an expert, but the truth was that these situations always made me feel a little uncomfortable. I opened the door of the car, walked across the gravel of the barnyard, took my hat off, and smoothed down my hair. The girl stood and waited patiently for me to come to her, looking off into the field where the men were working and idly adjusting her bonnet.

"Is your father around?" I said.

"He's out in the field there," she said, pointing without looking. "Did you come for the blueberries?"

"Yeah, I'm here for fourteen flats," I said.

"My mother set them out in the basement," she said. "Please wait here and I'll see that everything is in order."

She went back into the kitchen, and I could see the quiet movement of other people just barely visible in the cool dark behind her.

When she came back out the door, she had another little girl with her, an almost identical twin but slightly smaller. Each of them carried flats of blueberries. I went to meet them halfway across the yard and offered to take the smaller girl's stack, but she smiled politely and said, "That's fine," so I followed the two of them back across the yard to the car, feeling sort of useless. The older girl wrote out an invoice in neat, old-fashioned-looking figures with a stub of pencil. She was absorbed in her task and didn't make any small talk. When she was finished, she handed it over, thanked me politely, and they both went back inside.

The wind rustled the leaves in the walnut tree, and I could hear a cow complaining in the distance. A black van came up the lane and parked beside the barn. A man got out wearing pressed pants, a white shirt with suspenders, and the black porkpie hat that identified his particular sect of Mennonites. He stood by the van door, wiped his glasses with a handkerchief and folded it up again, lifted out a metal toolbox, and came around to where I was standing. "Did my daughter give you your blueberries then?" he asked. I said that she did. "All right then. We thank you. Tell your father that there will be more on Tuesday."

I got back in the car, and it smelled overwhelmingly like blueberries. Sarah didn't seem to have noticed any of the transaction; she had a pint of blueberries in her lap and had already eaten most of them.

"So, what's next?" she said.

I asked her if she noticed how cute the little girls were.

"Yeah, I guess, kind of weird though."

I was worried that not enough charm had rubbed off on her.

"These blueberries are really good," she said.

I figured that was good enough, put the car back in drive, and pulled out carefully so that I wouldn't scuff up the barnyard.

✳

From the Mennonite's farm we turned west and drove directly toward the wall of the ridge. We crossed more miles of rolling farmland and then made a sudden ascent, climbing a road built in wide switchbacks with long drops into the forest below. After a mile or two we crested the spine, and I pulled off to admire the view. To the east, the direction we'd just come from, there was a wide blanket of green and gold fields, cut square by thin roads, and to the west, the direction we were headed, was an endless series of wooded ridges, rolling off to the far horizon. Way below us, squeezed into the first valley, was the sooty glint of McConnellsburg.

The western side of these ridges—the side we lived on— had always, since the first settlers came here in the eighteenth century, been the wrong side. The Appalachian Mountains were the first real impediment to the western growth of the United States, and the geography—tight valleys and deep hollows—made the land difficult to farm and lonely to settle. There were still no significant cities in the two hundred miles between Harrisburg and Pittsburgh, a huge blank right smack in the middle of the Eastern Seaboard. It was the kind of country where people smoked generic cigarettes, let their aluminum siding go rusty and their aboveground pools collapse in the front yard.

It wasn't just the bad farmland that kept settlers away; the geography could also feel somehow sinister. Ten miles south along this ridge, outside the town of Shade Gap, a small town where I'd played Little League, there was an historical marker on Croghan Pike that noted that in the mid-eighteenth century the pioneers called this place "The Shadow of Death," because the Indians had killed so many settlers in the dark hollows. And in 1966—just ten years before my parents bought our land—a hermit known as the Shade Gap Mountain Man had kidnapped a girl, dragged her into the ridges above town, and held her in a cave for a week. After a massive manhunt he was shot to death in a barnyard near Fort Littleton. These were isolated incidents, and it obviously wasn't fair to judge the place by them, but it did lend a note of *Deliverance* that couldn't be totally ignored.

There were other problems here too, less visible to the naked eye, but lying close to the surface. A young man, feeling invisible out in his trailer at the end of a long dirt road, would overdose on the cheap heroin that had gotten easier to find in the last few years. An old woman would be convicted for selling pain pills and crack out of her ranch house on a back street, passing it to her customers through a torn screen in her bathroom window. A baby would be shaken to death by a drunken girlfriend, left unresponsive to drown in the tub. Later that fall I would see a friend from high school at a bar, and he would casually mention that a few weeks before he had watched his uncle fall drunkenly down the stairs and die on the ground in front of him. Certain tiny towns, way out in the hollows, eventually took on a sordid character, and glances from the people on the street would make a person hesitate to stop for gas. Like any place where opportunity was drying up, where some people felt uncared for and lonely, drugs sometimes seeped in to fill the cracks.

*

The geography was part of this feeling of strangeness, but there was also a culture gap, a basic lack of communication that had separated my family from many of the people who lived here. When I was little, a family lived in a trailer, just a few miles from the farm. All summer long they would sit at a picnic table in the front yard, just a few feet from the road. They were all very heavy, and there was always a pitcher of Kool-Aid on the table. It wasn't friendly, but we would laugh about them sometimes—how lumpy and boring they seemed—and they probably joked about us, the hippies who lived on the dope farm in Anderson Hollow. They knew that my parents were making a living as farmers, but they didn't know exactly how, and when they saw a pickup from our farm drive by with our employees, four young women in loose cotton dresses, or a man driving a rusted Honda with a guitar in the front seat, it must have seemed hard to believe that the success was due only to hard work. There was no real animosity between us, just a distance that nobody bothered to cross.

It was a particularly junky trailer, with long rust stains down the sides and a wooden landing at the front door that was pulling away from the structure. My parents didn't know the family and never had any reason to interact with them even though they lived only a few miles away. I knew the two boys who lived there though, because they rode the school bus and so did I. They both had identical bowl haircuts, and they were both minor bullies. The younger one was blond, with pale skin, and the bus driver called him whitey. The older one was more sullen, with an overbite and thin arms.

Every day during the summer, any time we went to town we would pass the whole family sitting out in front of the trailer, drinking Kool-Aid and smoking cigarettes. There were never any games or a radio—they wouldn't have gotten reception, anyway—and though there was a beautiful view of the open meadows across the road and the gentle ridge behind, they always faced away from it. It wasn't clear what they would do outside all day, but it was likely hot in the trailer, so they sat out there and watched the occasional car go by.

My mother often drove out for errands, so they saw her quite a bit. She may have tried to wave a few times at first, maybe even given a beep of the horn, but they never turned their heads, and eventually she just went past, and they acted as though they had never seen her. It was the same way one late afternoon in June when she took a few baskets of clothes and drove out the road to go to the Laundromat. I don't know if she noticed the little fluffy white dog playing in the dirt under the table, but I doubt she would have, because by now these people were invisible to her too.

When she drove home it was early evening. That stretch of road was notorious for deer, and she kept an eye out for the glint of their eyes where the headlights would reflect them. She drove slowly and saw that the family was still sitting outside. As she approached, the white dog darted out from under the table and ran into the road. My mother saw her just in time and came to a slow stop.

For a long minute everyone just sat. The people at the picnic table looked at her, and she looked at them, waiting for the dog to get out of the road. They didn't call to it, or make any motion at all, and my mother didn't want to get out of the car. She looked at the woman, maybe even mouthed through the windshield to ask if the dog had moved. The woman looked again at the road, and then at my mother. There was another long pause. The family went back to their conversation, and my mother sat and listened to the fuzzy radio. When she was sure the dog was out of the way, she pulled slowly ahead.

She felt a thump and knew immediately that the dog hadn't moved as she thought it had. The family got up from the table and came over to the road, and the husband picked the dog up off the asphalt. My mother was distraught, maybe a little frantic. She might have expressed bewilderment about why they hadn't said anything. The family might have asked her why she hadn't rolled down the window and yelled out to them. They didn't have this conversation though, because no one knew where to start. My mother, close to tears, apologized again, but the family just glared at her and went inside. My mother got back in the car and drove home.

✳

Sarah and I drove down the ridge and into town, past the cinder-block tattoo parlor and the motel that advertised its private showers in flickering red neon. The streetlights were just coming on, and people sat out on sagging porches in old lawn chairs, watching the traffic and smoking. Teenagers sat on the hoods of their cars, flirting under the yellow lights at the Bedford Petroleum station. It was July, but the tinsel from the town Christmas decorations had been left up and it glinted weakly. The convenience store in the middle of town was busy, the lot filled with shiny Ford F-150s and rusted-out Chevy Cavaliers.

I pointed out the little brick hospital where I'd been born, built behind a factory that made rawhide bones for dogs; the old theater where I'd seen my first movie, a matinee of *Coal Miner's Daughter*; and the old frame house where the library had been. I focused on how the pastures and cornfields came right up to the backyards of the houses, the old feed mill, and the sign that announced an ox roast at the fire station. We drove by a perfectly restored Farmall tractor that had been parked at the main intersection, the shiniest, newest-looking thing in town.

The town was losing pieces slowly, contracting into itself. For years a company called JLG had been a major employer, offering jobs building hydraulic lifts, but the global economy was damaging that kind of small manufacturer, and every year there were fewer jobs. The General Motors dealership sat vacant and blank, and the IGA had been sold to a discount bent-and-dent grocery store. The three oak trees in front of the courthouse had gotten sick and been cut down, and even the police station was out of business, closed after the sheriff put a notice in the paper and announced a public auction of the guns and the squad car. Unemployment in the county was among the highest in the entire state, and the most successful-looking business in town was the funeral home.

We left the main street and joined a smaller road and suddenly we were back in the countryside. We drove past a house with endless stacks of ice cream-colored beehives in the front yard and a barn with a faded sign that read: "Jane Fonda for President of North Vietnam." It got prettier as the evening came on, the setting sun filling the westward-facing windows of the houses with flaming orange, the valley cool and green, and the faint sickle of the white moon hung over the fields. We drove over the Aughwick Creek, where the trees bent over the water and the trout nipped at the flies gathering in the dusk.

When we were about ten miles away from home we passed the last business, an Amoco station with a bright sign, with a cloud of mayflies around it. Another mile beyond we turned left onto the Boy Scout Road, and the ridges rose up to either side and closed the road in completely, with just a line of brighter sky above us. Sarah's phone stopped working, so she turned it off and put it away. After five more miles we came out of the trees and into an open field where a herd of deer grazed in the new alfalfa, their eyes lit green and glowing in the headlights.

We cut off to the right onto Anderson Hollow Road. We bumped off the pavement, and the tiger lilies on the bank rubbed against the flank of the car. We drove past the first abandoned barn, where swallows rose up through the dark hole in the roof. Way off in the distance I could see the head-lights of another truck, picking its way along a ridge, and then it was gone over the opposite side and away from us. Sarah looked out the window and was quiet. We passed the shale cliffs, and the grove of trees, the dark shapes of cows wander-ing among the trunks.

I caught sight of our fields across the creek.

"There it is!" I said. "That's our corn!"

Under the open sky there was just enough light left to see.

"It looks really green."

I'd rolled the windows down now that we were almost home, and the air blew into the car.

"Everything's so green," she said, and then repeated it, almost like she was talking to herself.

We pulled into the barnyard, and I turned off the car. It was peaceful, everything quiet and put to bed for the evening. I parked by the lilac bush, sat for a long second, watched Sarah look around. Somewhere a screen door slammed, the sound of irrigation drifted from the field behind the barn. An apprentice in the summer kitchen laughed loudly and turned up the music, closed a door, and turned the shower on. Some-one was filling the tank on a pickup behind the shed and the crank on the pump made a heavy beat against the quiet whoosh of the surging gasoline.

We carried the flats of blueberries up to the cooler, swung open the heavy galvanized metal door, and stacked them beside a pallet of beets. The cold air smelled like dill, and I showed Sarah the rhubarb and the Italian parsley. I opened a box of fennel and another one of okra. She ate some raspberries from an open flat and some snap peas, and I moved things around so that we could get to the cases of beer that were stacked in the back corner. I grabbed two and opened them with the church key that hung beside the door.

We drank our beers and walked across the yard, through the fireflies in the unmowed grass. Through the screen door I could hear my parents at the table. The screen door suddenly flew open, and my mother ran out with a huge pot of boiling water that was too heavy to lift to the kitchen sink. She poured the steaming ears of corn out into the grass while one of the dogs nosed around. My mother pushed at the dog, juggled the scalding metal pot, danced around so that the boiling water wouldn't scald her bare feet. She yelled over her shoulder.

"Goddamn it, Jim, she just forgot, OK? It was hot as hell today."

My father's voice came back. "Well the carrots are all ruined. Ruined, split. I don't know why she doesn't care. No one cares."

"Oh, shut up," she said quietly to herself, then more loudly and back to the door, "They care, Jim. They all care."

A dog saw us and barked in our direction, then looked at my mother to see how concerned he should be about the stranger. She looked up, surprised.

"Hey! Jim, they're here!"

My father hadn't heard and kept talking.

"Do you know how many carrots there were out there? Do you? It's a total disaster."

My mother smiled at us and shook her head, then said more loudly, "Jim, Arlo and Sarah are home!"

＊

After a dinner of the corn, green beans, and slices of bread, my mother filled Sarah's arms with extra blankets, and we walked along the rutted track to the tent. The moon was high and hung in a gap in the trees. We cut through the high grass until we stood at the rim of the slope. I pointed out the little gap at the end of the field, and we went through it and down over the hill to the tent. The fireflies clung to all the blades of the grass and the crickets throbbed.

"Did you do this all by yourself?" Sarah asked.

"I just figured it out."

"Really? You just figured it out?"

That still sounded unlikely to me too, so I just let it sit. She paused before she stepped out on the floor.

"It's safe," I said.

We sat in the camp chairs and had a drink. A gnat drowned in hers, and I picked it out with the end of my pinky. Sarah set hers aside, so I drank both drinks down, and then we climbed into the tent and, eventually, into our sleeping bags. We lay there for a few minutes. Then she said, "It's really beautiful, Arlo. Really."

＊

I woke up an hour later and felt the space around me, running my hands over the soft walls of the tent, the ceiling, the unfamiliar shape of Sarah beside me, filling her normal side of the bed again. I unzipped the door and went out to the edge of the platform to pee. I could see the lines of the crops below me and smell the heat of the day rising up out of the field. When I climbed back in, Sarah shifted, and I knew that she was still awake. I asked her if she was worried, but she shook her head. I touched her cheek, and it was a little wet.

"Are you crying?"

She shook her head no.

"I'm just a little homesick. I'm being silly. I'm fine."

"We're going to have a good time, I promise."

"I know, I know."

6

The next day we woke up in the tent and stayed inside for a few minutes, talking quietly and enjoying the feeling of the very early morning. Sarah went out to pee in just her boots and underpants and squealed when the wet grass touched her bare bottom. I came out of the tent and stood on the far edge of the floor, looking down again on the field of cabbage stretching out in the mist. I looked around for Sarah, saw a flash of her white skin in the undergrowth behind the tent, and then she was back up on the platform, slipping her arms around me from behind and resting her cheek on my bare back. We stood there taking in the view, shivering and naked.

In the far distance we could see one of the apprentices coming along the dusty track beside the creek. He was bare-foot from wading through the ford on his way to work, with his pants rolled up to his knees and his lunch in a paper bag.

He was singing to himself. He stopped and looked closely at a few of the cabbages, checking for groundhog damage. Sarah looked down at herself and then at my nakedness.

"He doesn't know we're here," I said softly.

✳

We got dressed, went up to the barnyard, and ate a bowl of cereal in the kitchen. Sarah was wearing sunscreen, breathable fabrics in light colors, and a wide-brimmed hat. My mother came to the door, looking more like a real farmer. One leg of her cutoff shorts was slightly longer than the other, her T-shirt had a big bleach stain, and she was wearing her rubber boots. Her glasses were missing the right lens. An old butcher knife that she used to trim herbs was stuck in her waistband, and she was carrying a twenty-pound sack of dry cat food on her shoulder. She dropped the cat food on the porch, hooked the heels of her boots on the railing to pry them off, and came inside. She took three eggs out of her pocket and set them on the counter.

"You're going out to the barn, right? Pour some of this out for the cats. I'm going to eat breakfast."

Sarah opened the refrigerator door looking for something else to eat and came out with a block of cheese and a small linen bag. She held the bag in her hand, testing its weight. It made a dry sound, like it was full of small nuts.

"What's in here?"

"Ladybugs. They're in the fridge because the cold slows them down."

The bag started to move a little. Sarah opened it and poured a few beetles out on the counter. The bugs slowly crawled away. I stood up, picked up the escapees, and put the bag back in the fridge.

"They're for the greenhouse. They eat the aphids."

She sat down and drank her glass of milk.

Once we'd eaten breakfast we left my mother in the kitchen and walked across the gravel yard to join the crew. Everyone was gathering in the lower shed, milling around, putting on boots, and eating baked goods left over from Saturday market, talking and laughing with each other, petting the dogs. Two people were already absorbed in a problem with the tires on the watering tank while someone else was sharpening knives. A bandage on one of the dog's legs was coming unraveled, and someone was rewrapping it. People looked up when I introduced Sarah, said hello, and went back to what they were doing. I found a five-gallon bucket for her to sit on.

The barnyard always looked messy, crowded with tools and half-finished projects. There were iron poles propped in the long weeds against the barn wall, three dented oil drums outside the shed, a pile of broken wheelbarrows on the bank above us. There was a huge spiderweb crack in the windshield of the red Chevy, and the black Ford sat crookedly because it was missing a wheel. Weeds grew up everywhere they could—along the concrete walls and under the stairs. Someone had abandoned half of a blueberry pie on the counter, and a dog had gnawed on an ear of corn and then left it in the middle of the floor.

The crew leader came into the shed and handed around slips of paper that listed the plan for the day. People stood up and came to get one of the papers, eager to see the list of jobs. There was a long silence while everyone sat down to read. The plan had twelve lines for shared tasks and forty-four lines for individual ones, but the manager had run out of room, so she had filled the margins with them: make flats, harvest dill, harvest garlic, unload wood, harvest squash, transplant basil, burn trash, orchard pickup, move broccoli, lift potatoes, weed onions, trim garlic, cut shallots, pull drip tape.

Blight mitigation was also on the list. The disease was officially named *Alternaria solani*, a fungus that also affected potatoes. The spores germinated in as little as half an hour after entering a healthy field and only needed another two or three hours more to penetrate a plant, entering through small wounds or the stoma of the leaves. The first lesions appeared two days later, forming a bull's-eye shape. Infected leaves would turn yellow, and in three or four more days the disease would begin to affect the stems and the fruit itself. When it was fully mature, it created a black, velvety mass on the fruit, rotting it from the inside out and destroying the plant completely.

The week before, one of these bull's-eye lesions had been found in the first generation of tomatoes, the patch planted in Hortonville. The apprentice who managed the tomatoes had been scouting for problems and found the brownish-black mark in the east end of the field. Over the next few days he did more scouting and found more lesions, until it was clear that the entire patch was compromised. By the end of the week some sections had started to look sick, and the plants slouched in their trellis and wire supports.

My father took this news with a manic combination of res-
ignation and optimism. There were still three other patches
that hadn't been infected, and luckily the weather had stayed
bone dry, but every morning, while we sat at the kitchen
table and drank our coffee, we could hear the weather radio
on upstairs while my father brushed his teeth. At the end of
the week someone had used a big propane torch to burn the
sick plants down, leaving sections of black in the green rows.
With some good luck these measures might stop the disease
and contain it, and everything would go on as planned.

Now everyone started talking about the jobs at hand while
the crew manager assigned priorities. Someone made the argument that if the beans didn't get picked that morning they'd be
too big by the next day, and someone else said that her fennel
was getting chewed up by bugs and she needed three people to
get it out of the field now. The guy in charge of irrigation said
that the patch of beets on Hilltop West were dead and that it
wasn't his fault; he'd needed help the day before, but then he'd
had to go pick basil so the watering hadn't gotten done.

There was a sound of a phone being hung up, hard, and
then the screen door of my father's office slammed. Everyone
was quiet while they waited for him, picking at their scabs,
retying boots, finishing bowls of granola brought over from
the summer kitchen. He came around the corner of the milkhouse looking at a sheaf of notes on mismatched pieces of
paper. He stood in front of the group and read silently to
himself for a minute. Then he turned around and went back
to his office. Everyone waited some more. After a few more
minutes he came out again, stood in front of the group, and

looked surprised to see everybody. He had a distracted gaze that reminded me of old drunks—men always thinking about something else.

"OK. Who wants to start?"

He was dressed in a faded blue work shirt, khaki pants, and boots. The pocket of his shirt was full of pens, and there was a measuring tape clipped to his belt. His white hair was parted on the side and his neck was sunburned. He was holding an ear of corn that someone had brought up from Hortonville, which he'd shucked and then tasted to see how deep the kernels were and how many more days it needed in the field. Now he tossed the rest of the ear to a dog, who picked it up and carried it away to chew in private. He ran his hand through his hair and looked up again.

"Anyone?"

The apprentice in charge of irrigation said that the beets planted on the Hilltop were dead. My father didn't say anything, just shook his head and looked at his notes. Someone else said that the beans needed to come up today or they'd be too big.

"OK," my father said, like he didn't understand why they were telling him this.

"What's the problem?"

The manager mentioned that there was a squash pick to do and also the weeding in the onions, and there weren't enough people for the beans.

"Leave the onions," my father said.

The manager scratched it off her list.

"But it's got to be done tomorrow or it's going to be a disaster."

She put the onions back on another list.

"Anything else?"

Someone asked about the spacing of the kohlrabi.

"What did we do last year?"

There was a pause and then someone offered a guess of eight inches.

"Well, fifteen years ago we did it at eight, but I never knew why. Let's try twelve."

There was a general conversation for a minute, the conclusion being that they'd tried twelve inches and it didn't work.

"What about those kohlrabi on the Third Hump—what did we do with those?"

Someone spoke up and said those were the ones they'd tried to do at twelve inches. "Dave Doyle told me that he did it at twelve once, but I don't know. Maybe eight? What does the university extension say?"

It went on like this for five minutes, and eventually there was a decision to space half the patch at eight inches and half at twelve, compare the harvest, and note the better result for the next season.

The conversation turned to pest control. My mother had been finding nibbles while packing green beans, and an apprentice had gone down to the patch in the middle of the night with a flashlight to see if he could spot any mice. Potato seedlings had to be pulled up that had unexpectedly started sprouting in a crop of onions. Turkey manure that my father had bought for fertilizer had turned out to be full of weed seeds—even though the turkey farmer insisted the digestive process eliminated them—and they were suddenly germinating in the leeks. Grasshoppers were chewing up the basil and deer were trampling the beets. A copperhead snake had been spotted sunning itself in the cabbages, and hummingbirds were getting caught in the Japanese beetle traps.

The phone started ringing. My father yelled out into the barnyard, "Could someone get that, please?" but it didn't stop. Then a pickup truck pulled up and a man got out holding a gun and asked if he could hunt rabbits down along the creek. My mother yelled from the house that someone wanted to buy fifty pounds of rhubarb. Two of the dogs got in a fight over the ear of corn. Someone started to turn the motor over in one of the pickups, but it screeched and died. The driver tried again and the engine screeched again. There was a loud backfire and a cloud of bluish-gray smoke drifted into the shed.

People started getting ready to head out to the fields. The person who always wore a raincoat rummaged through the dusty ones hanging on the back wall and found the one she wanted. Someone else beat the dirt out of his wool hat, wrapped his neck in a dirty towel to protect it from the sun, and tied his dreadlocks up with a twist tie. People found their favorite knives and filled buckets with wrenches and propane torches. The radios clipped to everyone's belts were adjusted, already squawking with the tinny-sounding, abbreviated language of the crew.

✳

The work at the farm was hard. It was all physically demanding and especially difficult in the heat, and with the long days at the height of the summer, it could go on for thirteen or fourteen hours. It often caused lacerations and bruises, and every season someone went to the hospital with a deep cut or a broken finger. Sometimes it was worse. I still had a scar on my foot from the time it had been caught in a piece of equipment when I was four years old, a minor accident that could have been much more serious. The work could also be mindless and incredibly boring.

Sarah and I were assigned to pick okra. It wasn't a complicated job, but the apprentice in charge was very particular about how things were done. We went up to the barn, and I showed Sarah how to kick the boxes before she picked them up in case wasps had built nests there. I found two pairs of the clippers—German-made steel with orange handles—and I clipped a few hairs off my arm to check how fine the blades were. The apprentice came into the milkhouse and took his own pair of clippers from where he'd hidden them behind a jug of antifreeze.

The okra was particularly important to this apprentice. There was a certain amount of patriotism involved; he was from Senegal, and it was a traditional crop there. He'd also spent a huge amount of time experimenting with the crop. He had obsessively tracked the diseases and pests it was prone to, done elaborate comparisons of how the okra grew in wetter conditions or drier ones, how slightly different cultivation techniques and schedules affected it. He'd produced a stack of notes, research, and conjecture, and all of that work was expressed now in two long rows planted in the First Hump.

The field was right below the barnyard, and the plants were tall and spindly and swayed in the slight breeze. They had wide, toothy leaves and limp yellow blossoms with deep purple centers, stalks six feet tall and oddly articulated.

"There she is," the apprentice said, "my okra."

He stepped over to the plants and handled them gently, looking closely for bug damage, cut a pod off and held it up between two fingers so that we could see it. He put his pinkie next to it and looked at us.

"About that size."

Sarah held it to her own pinkie to note the size, and we started picking. After a minute I'd lost sight of her, but I could hear the snick of her clippers. The apprentice was working at the far end of the patch; I forgot about him and my mind drifted. Suddenly I felt a presence over my shoulder. It was him, watching me work. "Careful, careful," he said.

He checked Sarah's row too, holding the narrow stems between two fingers and moving aside the plants carefully, looking in the more hidden places. After a minute or two he came back with a big handful of ones she'd missed. Every few minutes he came back to offer unsolicited advice. He took Sarah's hand and showed her how to hold the clippers properly, and then he pointed out three pods that she'd just missed a minute before.

After forty-five minutes of work we got to the end of the row. We each had a box of the delicate little pods, green and fluted, bleeding a clear drop of moisture at the stem end where they'd been snipped. The apprentice shuffled his fingers through our boxes and picked out a bunch of pods that were too big or too small and threw them into the grass. He walked back toward the beginning of the row, looking at the plants we'd covered. He fluttered in the leaves here and there, snipping. We watched for a minute. He called out, "You missed some more," then looked over his shoulder and dismissed us, happy to be alone with his plants.

We walked by the chicken house on our way back and stopped to watch them fill the yard, beat up little dust baths, attack one another, peck in the weeds. We hooked our fingers in the chicken wire that surrounded the yard and hung there for a minute, stalling. I drank some of Sarah's water and took her box of okra so that she wouldn't have to carry it. I rubbed her neck for a second, and she pushed back against my hand. It was already getting hot. "Jeez," she said, "I was being careful."

The okra plants produced some natural chemical that irritated the skin, and our forearms were red and itchy from it. We scrubbed our arms as the apprentice came around the corner with the three boxes and set them on the table. He went through them again, picking out any stems or dead leaves, and put a sheet of clean white paper on top. He labeled the end in neat script and went back to hide his clippers.

"It's beautiful," he said and laughed. "I love this stuff!"

Sarah smiled weakly.

"You did a good job! You just need to learn, is all. You'll be an okra expert too, like me, I promise!"

✳

By now it was mid-morning, and the day was really hitting its stride. Jobs were all happening at once; someone was moving a pallet of seed into the barn with the tractor while someone else was filling tanks of gasoline. The squash pick was getting organized, and people were loading the wagon with empty boxes or sitting on the concrete wall, sharpening their knives. Sarah and I climbed up on the wagon with six others, and the driver started the tractor. There was a jolt when the wagon lurched forward, and everyone instinctively braced themselves against it except for Sarah, who suddenly grabbed my arm to keep herself from being thrown off.

If okra was tedious, then squash was a blunt, interminable slog, one of my least favorite activities on the entire farm. The summer squash—zucchini, sunburst, golden zucchini, and yellow squash—was one of the biggest volume crops, and it took hours to pick. It was harvested using a unique piece of equipment, a mechanical conveyor belt that set a steady, unrelenting pace. The plants themselves made it even worse—they were spiny and scratchy, so everyone had to cover up in long sleeves and pants despite the heat.

We bumped along, legs swinging over the sides of the wagon, and everyone else used the trip to relax, lying down in the dusty bed and looking up at the sky. One of the dogs had jumped up on the wagon, and she licked people's faces as we went down the hill, past the raspberries growing in the Pasture Patch and the cabbages that we'd been looking at earlier that morning when we first got up, and past some new corn in the Dogleg. The wagon dipped and rolled, and the people standing up kept their balance like they were on the deck of a ship.

When we got to the field, everyone jumped down and got

to picking, while the stronger people set up the conveyor belt. It was built on a frame made out of an aluminum extension ladder, a long strip of rubber connected to a motor. One end was braced on the floor of the wagon, and the belt was cantilevered thirty feet out to the right, over the rows. The pickers walked along with the belt in front of them and put the squash on it as they went. I found Sarah a good knife and showed her the ideal size. It wasn't hard to find the squash—it grew quickly and prolifically, a few on every plant—but even one extra day in the field let them grow too big.

Every vegetable on the farm was subject to a set of standards. For zucchini, each squash was required to be six to nine inches long, with a diameter of no more than two inches. The squash couldn't have any obvious dents or dings, and they were fragile, so they needed to be placed gently on the belt, almost like eggs. The stems had to be trimmed short, without cutting into the flesh, and the blossoms had to be removed. Any dirt had to be brushed off gently, and any obvious deformations—squash that were bent or had grown together like Siamese twins—were rejected. The ideal was consistency and quality. The person packing the squash threw away as many squash as he packed, and there was a thick layer of them on the ground on the road behind the wagon. Each vegetable, and often each variety, had its own standard. The crop manager learned them over time and tried to conform to the ideal.

These standards were developed by the USDA. Those for tomatoes alone filled fourteen pages, with hundreds of

subclauses, charts, and schematics that described the toler-
ances at measurements as small as a thirty-second of an inch.
A form, Visual Aid TM-L-1, detailed, in photographs, the
twelve variations in color that determined the grade of each
tomato. Defects like "shoulder bruising," "sunken scars," and
"cuts and broken skins" were all documented in detail. A
healthy tomato could be classified as "fairly well formed,"
"slightly rough," "reasonably well formed," or "misshapen,"
along with nine other classifications. "Puffiness" was noted,
along with "growth cracks," "hail," and any number of other
forms of damage. Each of these was calculated with complicated equations, and each had serious implications for how it
was shipped and marketed.

We didn't follow those as detailed as the official USDA
standards, but they were still very strict. Anything that was
sold through the co-op was subject to inspection upon delivery by the farmer, and vegetables were rejected on the loading dock all the time. A farmer would go home with fifty
pounds of basil because it was too wilted, or ten cases of carrots because they had too many cracks in the flesh. This was
serious business: often a chef would open a few random boxes
upon delivery, and if he found a rotten kohlrabi, he might
reject the whole order and never place another one. Maintaining standards was a key part of running a viable business,
and there was very little room for idiosyncracy.

The customers at our farmers' markets were less strict than
the wholesale market, but they still expected vegetables that
looked good. With some significant exceptions—lettuce got
bitter when it was large enough to bolt; the stems of basil

were woody if it was picked incorrectly—this mostly had to do with aesthetics rather than quality. Even so, it was an important point of pride. Opening a box of perfect eggplants, each one dark purple, none of the skins pierced with the sharp stems of the other fruit, all of them rounded, full, and evenly sized, was an indication that the farmer had done his job well.

Now the squash manager called out instructions to the crew and got ready to start. His job was to collect the squash as it came off the belt, sort it according to those standards, and pack it into boxes, which he then stacked on a pallet beside him. He finished preparing his station while the last people took their places in the rows. He nodded to the driver, the roar as the tractor started drowned out the sounds of the insects and the creek, and the belt started turning.

The tractor ground into gear and started to move forward, and the belt drifted away from us. Everyone immediately bent over and started picking, filling their hands with squash and dropping it onto the belt. Sarah suddenly realized how the process worked and bent down and started picking too, already a little behind. I beat the leaves around me gently and tried to pay more attention to the side of the row I shared with Sarah so that I could give her some breathing room.

The belt filled up quickly with squash, and the person on the wagon started packing them as fast as he could. His movements were brisk and efficient, like he was packing toothbrushes or auto parts, and the belt made a quick, rhythmic squeak. The squash kept coming, the boxes filled up, the stack on the pallet got taller, and the tractor kept crawling along.

Those of us in the field didn't talk or joke; we just kept our heads down and moved ahead.

After ten minutes or so Sarah was already falling farther behind, so I tried to pick more of her row before she was completely overwhelmed. The other pickers moved forward; there wasn't any easy way to jump rows and help someone else out, and soon both of us started chasing the belt, trying to make up the distance but only falling farther behind. The socks we were wearing on our arms itched, and we had to stop and pick gnats out of our mouths and eyes. The manager was keeping an eye on us, and after a minute or two he yelled to the driver to stop. Everyone else stood up and stretched for a minute while we caught up.

The tractor started to roll forward again as soon as we'd made up the distance between us and the belt. After twenty minutes though it suddenly made a choking sound and died. Everyone stood up at once and looked around, and the driver climbed down to look at the hydraulic hoses at the back. Crows called in the stand of pines to the north, and everyone started talking a little too loudly in the unexpected quiet, while Sarah and I worked to get ourselves completely caught up again. Sarah took off her hat and wiped her forehead, scratched at her ankles, and put her knife in her teeth so that she could adjust the socks on her arms.

She asked how much longer it would take, and I looked down the row toward the end and then back at where we'd started. I put my hands on my lower back and arched my spine, trying to loosen the muscles made tight by the constant stooping.

"Probably forty-five minutes more in this patch."

"This patch?"

"Yeah, there're two more."

"Seriously?"

Just when it seemed like the problem with the tractor might be significant enough for someone to run up to the barnyard for a tool or a part, there was a loud hiss and a small spurt of hot hydraulic fluid. The tractor started again, and everyone bent to the work. Sarah was doing better now, staying caught up for the most part, and I helped her when I could. I tried not to look up to see where the row ended; then, suddenly, there weren't any more plants in front of us, and the tractor died again.

I could hear the faint tinkling of ice cubes against glass. The driver was drinking deeply from the jar of water that she'd kept in the shade under her seat, and then she took off her sunglasses and rubbed her eyes, lifted her arms over her head, and flexed to each side like drivers do at rest stops when they've been watching the highway for hours. The pickers passed around another jug of water, and the person doing the packing stacked his boxes and counted things off, made some little notes in his book. When he was finished, everyone got on the wagon and sprawled around in the dust and the hay, and the driver started the tractor up again and headed to the next patch.

After two more hours of picking Sarah looked wrung out and unhappy. She scratched at her arms with the dull side of the knife, wiped the dust and sweat off her neck, and pushed her damp hair out of her eyes and behind her ears. When a dog nosed her hand Sarah didn't even look at her, just pushed her away and went back to examining her forearms. I asked her if she was feeling all right and she shrugged, so I gave her a little more water and let her be. Everyone was worn out and ready for lunch, and there wasn't much conversation on the ride up.

When we got back up to the barnyard, everyone dispersed. The dogs dozed in the shade under the pickup trucks, the bugs droned in the grass, and the air was still and hot. My mother always kept the doors and windows of the house closed to keep the heat out, so the kitchen was dark and cool. Sarah sat at the table, untied her boots, and stretched her feet. I cut some bread and cheese, set a jar of cold water on the table. We ate and drank quietly and then went upstairs to take a nap.

✳

Back at the shed that afternoon, a few people asked Sarah questions, about what she did in Massachusetts and where she was from originally, and there was more joking and general conversation now that we were on the down slope of the day. Two people played with a basketball at the busted hoop against the barn, one stomped out to three-point range and made a wild shot that sent the ball off into the pile of scrap metal beside the shed.

The manager organized everyone again, reassigned the priorities, and broke up the meeting. Sarah and I were doing irrigation, and I was happy because it was an easy job that would take up the rest of the day. The sun was at its hottest now, but the irrigation work involved working by the creek and getting wet; it was also just a straightforward job in general. The pipes got laid out in the field, we connected them to the pump, and the water got turned on.

The apprentice in charge went to the back of the shed and collected gaskets and latches, all of them slightly mismatched and in different states of disrepair. He picked up a sprinkler head and tested the spring, found an elbow joint and looked closely at the welding to see if it was cracked, checked a cap to make sure it was long enough to fit into the end of a pipe snugly. He took a few of each item so that he'd have some different options, and then the three of us went out on the Second Hump to collect the pipes. There was a big pile of them there, all baking in the hot sun, and I got Sarah an extra pair of gloves because I knew the pipes would be scorching.

The grass had grown over some of the older pipes at the bottom of the pile, so we had to work them free, tugging them from the ground and leaving behind a strip of yellow grass crawling with pillbugs. As I picked each one up, I tilted it and shook it a little in case anything had crawled inside. We scared up a rabbit and it took off across the meadow; its path was visible in the quivering tips of the tall grass. Once the pipes were loaded on the wagon we pulled them down to the Dogleg behind the tractor, the empty rattle of all the aluminum scaring the birds out of the trees.

We laid the pipes down the rows of corn. They were twenty feet long but light enough to be handled by one person, and we carried them over our heads like weight lifters, marching back and forth from the wagon to the field, until eventually there was a long silver line through the green shoots of the corn. We went back and connected them with the hook and latch on the end of each pipe, and then the apprentice picked up the last pipe and tugged so that all the connections along the line pulled tight.

We were moving quickly, and it felt good, covering the field in twenty-foot spans, huge leaps compared to the squash pick. Sarah seemed to be mostly recovered from that ordeal, and we were laughing and joking again, having fun. I lifted a pipe over my head and turned it like a giant helicopter blade, enjoying the force of it pulling strangely on my muscles. Sarah put her ear to one of the pipes while I ran down to the other end and whispered to her. She laughed for a second and dropped it, scratching at where the sound had tickled the bones of her face.

We waited while the apprentice went to get the pump started. He stopped and bent over to struggle with a connection for a second, then sat back on his heels and looked down the line of them. He rubbed his forehead and stood up.

"They're all backward," he yelled down to us.

We walked back to the beginning of the line and unlatched them all, picked them back up over our heads, and dropped them again.

When we were done, we all walked down to the creek together. The water flowed by, cold and deep, and the green plants that grew among the rocks shivered in the breeze. The apprentice cranked on the lever that primed the pump, adjusted various screws, knobs, levers. When he reached down and turned the key, there was a giant explosion as the pump backfired. Sarah's hands flew up over her ears, and we all jumped backward. The pump sat there, completely dead, and we watched it for a second while the sounds of the creek resumed. "Shit," the apprentice said.

He went back and made some more adjustments and tried again. He turned the key until there was another small explosion; then he took one of the shields off the motor and rubbed some grease away and tried again. Nothing happened; the pump just sat there brooding. Eventually the apprentice went back up to the barnyard to get a socket wrench, and the pump coughed, then sputtered, and eventually caught, the whole shuddering bulk of it coming to life and shaking so hard that it seemed it might come apart.

A little whirlpool appeared in the water over the intake pipe, the pipes farther up the hill started to bang, and water spurted out of the loose connections. The apprentice was only three feet away, but it was so loud that he cupped his hand around his mouth and shouted at me, "It's good, it's good!" and I ran up the hill to see if the water was making it farther down the line. Sarah came with me, and we both stood and watched.

There was no water in the field, so we scouted the line until we found a leak. We fixed the connection and went down to the end of the field while the apprentice started the pump again. There was a deep gurgling sound and then a solid column of water came gushing out and soaked our shoes. I got down on my knees in the mud and wiggled the cap into the end of the pipe, but it was the wrong size, so the apprentice got back on the tractor and went speeding back up the hill to get the right one.

The water finally started its slow march up the field, the sprinklers coming on one by one. At the third sprinkler from the end, it suddenly stopped. I got a wrench and beat on the sprinkler, tried adjusting the screw that determined the tension, and finally I put my mouth on it and blew. I found a piece of wire and stuck it into the brass fitting, worked it around. The obstruction was soft, probably a wad of straw. I pushed some more, dug deeper, and all at once the sprinkler spouted blood. It sprayed across my shirt, dark crimson on white cotton. I jumped back.

"What is that?" Sarah said.

I looked at the blood and at the end of the wire.

"It's a mouse I think."

We took the sprinkler head apart and took out the little smashed corpse. The apprentice started the pump again, and suddenly everything was working beautifully. The spray of water fanned out in the late sunshine, and the trees along the creek made a green backdrop; the sky was bright blue and just verging on navy at the edges. I took off my boots and walked out into the wet field, letting the sprinkler water soak my T-shirt, tipping my head back so drops could fall on my face. It smelled like dust, metal, and cold water. The sprinklers turned in a syncopated beat, and the falling water rinsed off the heat.

✳

We went back up to the barnyard and put away the tools, and then Sarah and I sat on the lawn and shared a beer. My mother was down below us, hoeing thyme plants in the cool early evening. We talked among ourselves, calling out to my mother now and then, half listening to the soft scuffle of her hoe in the dirt.

We saw a deer come out of the pink and purple dame's rocket, lit by the last of the sun, and move back into the dark shade of the trees. A dog came and warmly nuzzled my hand, flopped on her back, stretched all her paws, grunted with pleasure while I scratched her belly. Another came, jealously. I smelled the lilacs and the roses, the rosemary. I stretched my legs, felt all the muscles of my feet.

Sarah lay back in the grass and threw her arm over her eyes. I asked her if she was happy. She wasn't sure.

❋

When I was still working in the museum, every project had a checklist, a clear set of milestones. I worked until I satisfied these requirements, and then I put the project away. On the farm, though, we were immersed in the summer, a wide, warm ocean with no shore in sight and no landmarks to swim toward. Now we rested in that same ocean, floating as it moved around us.

A few years after Bert had died, Lina made a charcoal drawing of a man working in a furrowed field. She wrote a line of text across the image, explaining how he'd loved to make his rows of beans especially long. The other people working with him would complain; they wanted a series of shorter rows rather than just a few longer ones, but Bert insisted. She wrote that he didn't like the idea of having the goal so close by, didn't want to think about the end, didn't want to plan for the future, that he wanted to pick what was right in front of him without worrying about the asparagus to be weeded or the leeks to be dug.

I considered this sometimes when I thought about the age of my parents. Most people in their mid-sixties were winding things down in their professional careers, looking toward a future of golf or gardening, maybe a move to a smaller apartment, creating a safe enclosure for their lives that they'd earned over decades. What would my parents do when they were ready to stop? There was no way that they could just finish being farmers, close things up and walk away, move on to different tasks. They were the farm and the farm was them, and to separate the two would be impossible.

*

A week later Sarah and I were at one of the potlucks that were held every Wednesday on the farm. There was generally a theme, some selected vegetable for everyone to cook with, and that night it was carrots. Everyone gathered around— curried carrots with peas, a carrot casserole with whole wheat bread crumbs, a cold salad made from vinegar and shredded carrots, a stir fry of bitter carrot greens that everyone avoided, carrot bread, and a big glass jar of carrot juice. There were loaves of bread and bottles of beer and a big plate of carrot sticks.

Sarah was dressed the same as everyone else now, a dirty T-shirt and stained pants tucked into a pair of green rubber boots. I sat at the other end of the table and watched her as she threw a yellow squash out into the yard for one of the dogs to fetch. She was laughing and drinking a beer, and her skin was brown and tan. She looked beautiful.

Someone asked what was in the casserole, and the person who'd made it mentioned oregano. Sarah had been weeding that and doing the harvest, taking responsibility for the small patch that grew in the garden.

"You hear that? That's your oregano," my mother said to Sarah.

"I know! How is it?"

"Fine. It's oregano," my mother said.

"Do you think that it's getting enough water? It was pretty wet on Monday, but then it got so hot, I wasn't sure. And it had some yellow at the bottoms of the plant."

She and my mother talked about it for a minute or two more, just another conversation around the table.

That night we walked back down over the hill to the tent, and I told Sarah about my plans to build a roof on the platform so that we would have more room. She snuggled up against me and said she didn't mind sleeping in the tent.

7

By August we'd entered the part of the season when the work felt mindless and everything was a chore. In the morning the air in the tent already felt hot and close, and we walked up toward the barnyard without talking much. In the distance we saw an apprentice coming out of his cabin, but we didn't call out to him, just watched as he trudged up the hill like us. Eventually our paths intersected, and we walked the last part together, past the back of the barn where the cats sat in the broken windows. The road was dusty, and the morning was already hot.

The crew was always burnt out by this point in the season. The morning meeting was quiet and without much joking; someone drew in the dirt with the toe of her boot and another idly pulled on a dog's ears until she yelped. The crew leader was handing out the plan of the day, and everyone just waited for the sheets to come around to them. The list was full, as it had been for weeks. There was a harvest of corn and celery, the shallots had to be brought into the barn to be laid out and cured, and we needed to transplant broccoli. My father didn't leave his office, just talked to the field manager alone for a few minutes, and then stayed at his desk going over invoices.

In the last few weeks the tomato blight had showed up in the second generation of plants. My father was already taking a certain satisfaction, saying that he'd predicted it all along, that he knew that we'd never be able to stop it, that we probably deserved it anyway for not being careful. A villain had been identified—a rumor was going around among growers that the blight had been spread all along the East Coast through shipments of plants that went to the nursery sections of Walmarts and Home Depots. But my father also laid blame closer to home. He told the apprentices that they hadn't been careful enough, that they hadn't done everything they could to control it, and—worst of all—that they just didn't care.

He'd ended up apologizing to the crew the next day because the truth was that however the blight had gotten there, and however it had spread, there just wasn't much we could do about it. The spores were in the wind, and they germinated in the dew. Every drop of rain was a potential vector for disease, and every morning mist was an incubator. If we were a conventional farm, the blight would be a distraction—it would be easy to carpet bomb the infection with chemicals—but there were no special organic techniques and no way to stop the rain that would let it thrive. We would probably lose the first two generations, so we put our hopes in the last two, which were still healthy.

As the meeting broke up, a tractor chugged out of the mist that lay near the bottom. The crew of five people riding along had been picking corn for two hours already, starting at six, when it was still cold and the corn wouldn't get ruined by the heat. They formed a line and passed the bags of ears off the wagon and into the packing shed, where they would spread them out on the concrete floor of the cooler. The person standing on the concrete dock caught the sacks as they were thrown across the gap, handling them like mailbags, absorbing the forty pounds of them with his body and stacking them on pallets. Afterward they would take a break to eat breakfast. Everyone else headed off to get their day started.

No one gathered in the barnyard for beers and conversation after work. Everyone wanted to be by themselves. Sarah and I sat on the back porch with our eyes closed and listened to the cicadas hum like electric wires. Dinner was tense. My father came in and didn't say much. He just washed his hands and got a beer, sat down at the table and sighed, waited to eat. After dinner Sarah, my mother, and I played a game of Scrabble that none of us had the energy for. Eventually my mother went up to bed, and Sarah and I walked back out to the tent, passing the lit window of my father's office. We could see him in his pool of light, worrying.

✳

That night Sarah and I decided to take a break for a few days. Not for very long, just a weekend, but we were going far enough away that we could feel a real separation from the farm. We decided to drive to New Hampshire, to a cottage on a lake that had been in my mother's family for more than a century. We could swim there, go for long walks in the mossy woods, and spend hours reading in the wicker rocking chairs. There was a phone in the house but not much else, just big empty rooms filled with mismatched furniture and a long porch that looked out over the silent lake.

My mother and her six brothers and sisters had spent their summers in the cottage. Each year the family got a moving van and took everything—linens, dishes, and wardrobes— the ten miles out of town to the cottage and left my grandfather to stay behind and work in the courthouse, where he was a judge. He would come out to the lake on the weekends, leaving his stifling office full of cigarette smoke and paperwork, and paddle a canoe around for an hour and then have a gin and tonic. He died when my mother was only five years old, but she still remembered him during those summer evenings, relaxed and comfortable, free of his troubles at work and surrounded by his big, happy family.

When I was growing up, decades later, my sister and I would go to New Hampshire with my mother every August, and the cottage had most of the same furniture in it and even the same dishes. It was a hard time for my mother to be away from the farm, but she did it anyway, figuring that New Hampshire and the cottage were too important a part of our family history to give up completely, and that we needed a break from Pennsylvania. In all those years we always left my father behind. He couldn't relax there like my grandfather had. There was just too much to do at home, too much corn to pick and too many tomatoes, too many small emergencies that only he could fix.

✳

On Friday night Sarah and I showered and packed two small bags with some of the clean clothes that we hadn't worn for weeks. The drive was eight hours, through sodium-lit New Jersey and leafy Connecticut. We drove over the New Hampshire line just as the sun came up, and we were at the lake thirty minutes later. I shook Sarah awake gently and told her we were there. Then I got out of the car, took off my clothes on the dock, and dove into the glassy water, startling a family of ducks sleeping on the wooden float moored in the deep water. I hoisted myself out, dripping and clean, and lay on the boards to take a long nap.

There was another reason I wanted to make the trip. I was also going to visit Chloe, Bert and Lina's daughter, who was just six months old when Bert died. She lived in Maine now, just a couple hours' drive east. On Sunday I planned to drive over with Sarah to talk with Chloe about Blue Moon. She had left when she was still a baby, and I didn't know how much she knew about what her parents had done there, but I wanted to tell her what I could remember about the farm. She was the last of the original inhabitants of that farm; her mother, Lina, had died of cancer the summer before. It seemed important for me to express my admiration for her parents and for what they had accomplished. I didn't know if it would be any help to her, but it seemed like a small but useful way to honor the memory of Bert and Lina.

✳

One of the things that had always seemed most important about New Morning was that our whole family was involved in it. Part of this was simple proximity; at any time during the day my father was in his office beside the barn or in the fields below the house, and my mother was in the basement sorting eggs or in the packing shed at the top of the barnyard. It could be claustrophobic, especially when things were going badly, but it was also comforting to know that my parents were always close by if I needed them. We were all in it together, for better or worse, and when I was little I never realized that this arrangement of family and livelihood was unique.

By owning the farm and growing it successfully, my parents had taken us on an adventure with them. If I went to my friends in Massachusetts now, men and women in the prime of their careers as investment bankers and tax attorneys, owners of excellent credit and houses in good school districts, and said that I was starting a farm on borrowed money, committing to the job of growing vegetables for the rest of my life, they would be embarrassed for me. They would think that I was giving up on real life for a fantasy, and they might have secretly congratulated themselves; I'd be broke and missing five years on my résumé by the time I came to my senses. The idea of having a kid in the middle of nowhere, in some sad, primitive hospital without even a full-time obstetrician, they would have considered the height of irresponsibility.

And it was a little irresponsible, when my parents did it, in a way. I'd been born at the end of March during a blizzard that could have trapped my pregnant mother at the end of our dirt road. I was delivered by a GP, who still worked at the same hospital in McConnellsburg where I'd been born, setting broken fingers and prescribing antidepressants. My parents had brought me home and put me to sleep in the bare upstairs bedroom with the rattling windows and the crumbling plaster, sang to me while they planted basil, changed me while they picked the first asparagus, and despite the pneumonia I got when I was eighteen months old from splashing in the cold creek, I lived. Five years later they did it again and had my little sister.

✳

Sarah and I spent a couple of quiet and uneventful days at the lake; we woke up early with the sun. We took the canoe out and paddled in the shallows, stopping along the granite shoreline to fill the bottom of a coffee can with the wild blueberries that grew there. We drove a few miles to the movies in Brattleboro and to a batting cage in Swanzey, where Sarah was scared of the ball, and I pretended that I wasn't. We went to a farm stand and bought green beans and corn, not as nice as our own, and secretly judged the farmers for seeming too relaxed.

On Sunday we closed the house back up, got in the car, and headed east toward Portland, Maine. On the way we drove through the city where my mother grew up, and I gave Sarah a tour of my family history—the mill with my great-grandfather's initials on the smokestack, my mother's elementary school on School Street, the Unitarian church. Finally we drove to Court Street and looked at the big brick house where my mother had lived as a teenager. Ivy climbed the brick and there was a gold pineapple carved above the red front door. It was easy to imagine all my aunts and uncles sitting in the yard under the elms, my grandmother meeting with her bridge club, my stepgrandfather in his office at Wright's Silver Cream, the company his own grandfather had founded.

My mother hadn't been particularly satisfied with the options that life in that house presented, and that's why she'd taken a train down to Sleepy Creek when she was twenty-six to go on a blind date with my father. She loved her family, but she didn't feel comfortable with the expectations of how she should comport herself in that small town where her family was so prominent. She didn't like the drinking and clubbiness that was part of that world, and she didn't want to spend her days having drinks with her cousins at the country club or going to cocktail parties at other people's lake houses. She had kept a few souvenirs, though, including a jeweled ashtray she still kept on her desk, and once in my uncle's apartment in Boston I'd asked about a silver dollar he kept on his bookshelf, one side silver and the other painted light blue. After the house on Court Street was sold, he had snuck back in the middle of the night with a hammer and chisel, climbed down to the bottom of the empty swimming pool, and chipped it out of the place where it had been set in the concrete since 1934.

✻

We drove out of town and across the state on the two-lane road that transverses New Hampshire and goes to the coast.

Eventually we got to the ocean and headed north, leaving the bigger roads and taking a route that went through the salt marshes and past rocky beaches. There were farms there, the fields plowed almost right up to the ocean, and they were full of corn now. Over the tassels we could see the glinting water and the neon buoys that marked the lobster pots, and the white boats in the distance, puttering between them.

Eventually we found the house on Seal Cove Road. I drove past it and pulled into an ice cream stand down the road, turned off the car, and sat for a minute. Sarah put her hand on my arm. I was nervous because I still didn't know exactly what I was going to talk about with Chloe. Sarah was sure that she would be eager to hear about her parents, but I wasn't sure that I could tell her anything important about Blue Moon. I felt like the little stories and anecdotes I had to offer might seem silly and pointless to her.

We drove back to the house and pulled into the driveway. I parked under a huge old tree that shaded the lawn and turned the car off. It was a beautiful house, white clapboard and built in a style that's re-created in subdivisions all over the country but only really belongs in Maine. While we sat there, a golden retriever came bounding across the lawn, barking happily, and it occurred to me that whoever was in the house knew we were there and that it would be strange to sit there any longer. Sarah and I went up onto the porch, and I knocked. We could hear someone walking to the door. It opened, and Chloe was standing there smiling in a way that I recognized from pictures of Bert.

She was blond, small, and pretty in a way that seemed

familiar. For years there had been a photograph of Chloe stuck in the edge of the frame of Bert's funeral announcement in our kitchen, and even though she was probably six or seven years old in the picture, and was twenty now, I could still match that girl to the one in front of me—the same downward tilt at the corners of her eyes, the mouth and nose that came together the way her father's had. She held the door open so that Sarah and I could come in.

I said hello and introduced Sarah, and we all hugged and made small talk about the drive. Her stepfather came to the door as well, a big man with a walrus mustache and a soft voice, and I told them both how sorry I was about Lina. They thanked me and led us into the kitchen, offered us lemonade. I looked around at the paintings on the walls, most of them by Lina. I recognized them from the rooms of that old house at Blue Moon. They were bright and cheerful, and I was happy to be able to say that I knew them.

I stopped by one piece of art that I didn't remember, different from the others, a print with a photograph and a line of heavy text. The black-and-white picture at the center was of Lina's grandfather, standing on his own farm in the Midwest. The text said: "The Great Depression in Nebraska. No money. No feed. To 'help,' the government bought my grandfather's registered Holsteins for $13 a head then shot them. My grandfather almost lost his mind."

We went outside on the weathered wooden deck and looked out over the marshes toward the ocean beyond. A line of wild turkeys came out of the high sedge, and we sat watching in silence, sipping cold drinks. The road that ran in front of the property was quiet and a couple of other houses were visible, all neat and well kept, with green lawns and mature trees. I thought that it would have been a nice place to grow up. Portland, with its pretty streets, its stores and galleries, was only a few miles away, and there would be plenty of other kids around to play with. The ocean was nearby, and there was probably a town beach with frigid water.

After a few more minutes of small talk I started to tell Chloe what I remembered about Bert and Lina, and everything I knew about Blue Moon. I told her about the springhouse and about the rooms in the house with the wasps' nests and about the bonfires. I told her about the time her mother had set up a maypole in the yard and had everyone dance around it with streamers. I told her how her parents had organized a protest in the county seat, and how they had made those giant puppets of black vultures, and how the puppets had eventually been left in our own barn.

I talked and talked, and as I went on, I started to feel a little desperate. I wanted to explain what it felt like in Pennsylvania, how beautiful it was but also how lonely. She listened carefully to what I was saying and asked questions now and then. I told her how I remembered Bert had built and flown rice paper kites on the hill above the barn, and how we used to go to Blue Moon for tobogganing parties when it snowed. I found every happy memory I could of Bert and Lina and trotted it out. Somehow though, I was still missing the point, something more complicated than a bunch of stories about sleds and bonfires.

✳

My father has a picture in his office of me sitting at the wheel of our John Deere, the second tractor he bought after the Model C. I'm four years old, blond and tan, and I'm smiling at the camera. There's the perfect green color of the tractor's hood, combined with the bright yellow of the front forks, and me in the middle, one hand on the wheel and smiling wildly. I don't remember the picture being taken, but it's a fairly typical pose. It's a picture that a lot of farmers take of their kids, a reminder of a childhood spent on a farm and evidence that it was a good way to grow up, a childhood full of sun and playing in the fields and fresh vegetables.

The truth was that I had always felt more ambivalent about the farm than that picture might have let on. By the time I was fifteen and old enough to really understand how much of the rest of the world I was missing, I started to lobby my parents to send me away. This eventually landed me at a boarding school. It wasn't too far from home, just an hour, but if anything I would have liked it to be more distant. I did miss my parents and my sister, but the school, with its stone buildings and old trophies, just seemed like a more appropriate place than the farm for the person I wanted to become.

In my sophomore year my father had come to my dorm unexpectedly one afternoon, stopping by on his way home from market. I'd missed him, and the boy who lived in the room next to mine told me that a man wearing boots had been looking for me. He'd assumed it was a maintenance man, and I didn't tell him that it was my father because I was embarrassed. When Parents' Day came around later in the school years, our car was the only one in the lot behind the dorm that was dusty, the backseat full of tools, straw, and cardboard boxes. When they suggested we drive to dinner, I told them I'd rather walk.

✳

Chloe went inside and brought out a box. It was small, about the size of a loaf of bread. She opened it, and I leaned forward, then caught myself and leaned back so she wouldn't feel that I was snooping. She handed me things one by one: a watercolor of two old gloves that Lina had painted, a picture of Bert with the fields behind him, an announcement that said, "We're Moving to a Farm in Pennsylvania!" The last thing was a picture of her as a baby, clipped from our local newspaper. She was sitting on a table at a farmers' market, surrounded by baskets of peppers and chives. She held a bunch of flowers in her hand, offering them to the camera in a pudgy fist.

The farm was everywhere in these reminders from childhood. Later that summer I was going through the bookshelf in the living room of my parents' house, flipping through a copy of *Rabbit, Run,* full of the notes my mother had written in the margins for her freshman English class at Skidmore College, smart and witty and in the exact same handwriting she still wrote in now. I read some of the beginning of the Updike, the section where Rabbit flees his chubby new baby and his thin, drunk wife.

In the back of the book I found a slip of cardboard that someone had used to mark their place. It was three inches by two, slightly yellowed, and it had sharp black print that seemed slightly old fashioned. There was a line for a room number and another for blood type, and the name on the card was "Baby Girl Crawford." It was the identification from my sister's bassinet in the hospital in McConnellsburg. I looked at the card for a second, wondering at the weirdness of it, and then I flipped it over. There, on the back of the card in the same neat script, my mother had made a list of things to take to market the next Saturday after she got home from the hospital: "cash boxes, aprons, peach crates."

※

After more small talk, I decided that I would try and address something that had been nagging at me. I hadn't really brought up what had actually happened to Bert, and it seemed like I should offer some sort of explanation.

"You know, it was really hard for your parents to do what they did. Pennsylvania, way out there in the middle of nowhere, is pretty bleak. What happened to Bert, your father, was . . . Well, I used to worry a lot."

I started to cry. I kept smiling at Sarah and Chloe both, making expressions that I hoped conveyed how silly this was for me to be doing, and how I was mystified by it myself. I would get settled, look out toward the ocean again, and try and focus on some distant point, and when I would turn around, it would come again, like a hiccup. Chloe didn't seem uncomfortable. She shrugged, said "That's OK," and waited for me to stop. It occurred to me that she was probably getting used to people crying in front of her.

I was thinking about how Bert had been shot and how much that had scared me at the time. I was thinking about myself, as a twelve-year-old, and how much that event had made me fear for my own parents' safety. I was thinking about how I had always felt more comfortable sleeping at night with a sword and how scared I'd been of what might come out of the dark. Bert's murder had confirmed all my worst fears, that we were living in a dangerous place where we didn't belong. We would always be outsiders there.

✴

When I was very little, starting at age three or four, my parents would leave me with local people in Pennsylvania when they went to market on Saturday mornings. The first of these babysitters that I can remember were three spinster Mennonite sisters who ran an egg farm. My parents would drive down their long driveway in the early morning dark, and one of the sisters would come out in a nightgown and bonnet to collect me. She would take me into the stone house and put me back to sleep in a huge, heavily carved bed with a sepia-toned picture of Jesus over the headboard. In the morning, the sisters would bring me with them while they did chores, doting on me.

When I was just a little older though, I would stay with a woman who lived closer to the farm. She had two kids of her own, a boy and a girl about my age, and we would spend the day together playing in the woods behind the house or across the road in a big open meadow where there was an old well, collecting rocks and dropping them down to hear the splash at the bottom. The house next door burned down one night, and we spent the next week exploring the burnt wreckage, collecting scorched survivors from among the victim's belongings.

My babysitter's husband worked away from home all day, in a garage in town. He would come home in the late afternoon, and if my parents hadn't picked me up yet, I would spend an hour or two with him, staying through dinner if it got late. He terrified me. He wore the smoked glasses that were popular at the time, and he had a Fu Manchu mustache that draped around his mouth. He wore a welder's cap, a cloth beanie with a tiny brim, and he had long arms that were greasy up to the line of his T-shirt. His shitkicker boots had flat front toes, and he drove a pickup with chrome pipes.

He would eat as soon as he came home, deer bologna with yellow cheese and white bread, or country ham and dumplings, and then he would sit in a recliner in the living room, watching *MASH* and *Happy Days*, drinking Pabst Blue Ribbon and smoking. He never had much to say, and he talked in a high Appalachian whine that I could barely understand. His cigarette ash would drift into the shag carpet, and the Pabst bottles would collect on the oak table beside the chair, and eventually he would rouse himself and go to bed. We moved quietly around the house, careful not to wake him.

The fact that he beat his children with a belt never seemed particularly important at the time. It was a standard form of discipline, not much different than the wooden pad-dle that all my elementary school teachers used. The mother never used the belt, but it hung on a nail in the kitchen, and even minor transgressions, refusing to eat the cold, cut-up hot dogs that we were served for lunch, or just talking back, were met with a "wait until your dad gets home."

There was a dog in the house, a little dachshund mix with milky eyes and a slight limp, but one day a neighbor dropped off another dog, this one black and larger. The dog was imme-diately named Blackie, and like most dogs in the area it was chained to a house in the backyard, left to wear a circle of dust and to sleep in the depressions in the dirt worn out by the constant pacing. When the father came home with a few groundhogs that he'd shot, he skinned them and threw the dog the steaming guts.

Over the next week the son played with the dog, but then he lost interest. This would have been the end of the story, except for the fact that the dog barked. Constantly and with-out good reason, and in a way that couldn't continue. The boy, my friend, sometimes took him off his chain, and the dog would run around happily and in silence until he was tied up again. When the father got home, it became more serious. That night he sat at the kitchen table, scooping up his mashed potatoes and glaring at the wife. She yelled out the back door, but the dog didn't stop.

In the morning before he'd left, the father had warned the son about the barking. We spent the day climbing up a crum-bling dirt bank behind the house, playing with a Rambo knife that had a compass on the butt and a hidden compartment that held fishhooks. The dog barked and the boy yelled at him: "Shush, Blackie, shush!" I asked him what he was going to do, and he said, "I'm gonna get licked." I was scared for him, but he didn't seem too worried.

The father came home that night and sat down to dinner. There was silence in the house, and the dog kept barking. The father looked at the son, and the son looked back down at his plate and pushed his corn around.

"What in the hell did I tell you about that damn dog?"

The barking continued, and there was nothing anyone could do about it. The father set down his fork and looked around the table.

"Well?"

He pushed his chair up and went down the dark hallway to the bedroom he shared with his wife. When he came out again, he was holding a rifle. He pushed the back door open and walked up to the doghouse. We sat at the table and listened, and the dog started barking more frantically as he approached, there was a single shot, one small yelp, and the dog was dead. The son went to his room to cry, and dinner went on.

In retrospect the whole incident had a certain logic. The man had a dog that he couldn't keep and that he didn't know what to do with. There was no one else who would take it, and no way to change its behavior. To have tied the dog up, taken it out to some lonely place and shot it there, or just left it to run wild would have been a waste of time. The dog was going to die one way or the other, and it might as well have been then.

I don't remember talking to my parents about this, but my

visits to that babysitter got less frequent. My sister got older, and we started staying with another family more often, on a farm where they raised turkeys and shorthorn cattle. The wife served us something she called cracker soup for lunch, saltines crushed into warm water and melted margarine, and we both loved it. Eventually my sister and I grew up and there was no more need for babysitters at all.

✳

I finished telling Chloe my happier stories about her parents, more collected now, and she put the box of mementos away. We went around the back of the house and looked at Lina's garden, big and full of flowers in bloom and neatly divided into separate beds. It was beautiful, and Sarah and I both said so, gushing a little and maybe making a bigger deal of it than Chloe had meant for us to. She accepted the compliments and said how much her mother had loved growing those flowers, because it reminded her of being a farmer all those years ago.

I'd been talking so much that Chloe hadn't had much of a chance to say anything. Now she told me about the one time that she and her mother had gone back to Blue Moon, about how run-down the place was, how there was rusty machinery everywhere. She said that there were animals running free, turkeys and goats, and it seemed wild and chaotic. She talked about how rough the house was and how the rooms had seemed cold. She wasn't complaining, just telling me what she'd seen. The only time she sounded disappointed was while talking about the greenhouse and how much it had bothered her mother that the windows were broken.

Chloe told me more about herself, that she'd recently won a prestigious prize that was presented to her in Carnegie Hall and been accepted to art school in Chicago. She was friendly in a way that made me comfortable; she seemed sure of herself and spoke confidently about things that were important to her, all personality traits that she shared with her father, though I didn't tell her that.

We got ready to leave, and I told Chloe that if she ever wanted to come to Pennsylvania, she was welcome to visit my mother and father and that they could tell her more than I could about what her own parents had done at Blue Moon. They could even go over there with her and show her around if she wanted, explain everything in detail. She was appreciative, said thank you and that she might do it sometime, that she'd love to see our farm too. I knew that she probably wouldn't though.

The truth was that Chloe might have already had everything she needed from Blue Moon in that shoe box. A story of what her parents had done during those years could be teased out of that material—the sketches of the two old gloves, the invitations to the parties, the photographs. The land itself wasn't really all that important; it was just fifty acres of fields and forest, with a stream running down out of the ridges. She could take what she wanted, decide for herself how important it was that her parents had been farmers.

*

We got back in the car. I honked as I pulled out of the driveway, and Chloe waved back at us and went inside. We were quiet for a long minute or two, and then Sarah put her hand on my leg.

"How do you think it went?"

"Fine."

"I love you, you know."

"I know."

"I think Chloe was really glad that you came."

"I guess so. Thanks for coming. I feel really stupid that I cried like that."

"Don't be ridiculous," Sarah said. "It's a sad story."

Sarah and I drove home that afternoon, back to New Morning. When we pulled in that night, the dogs all started barking, and when we got out of the car, they surrounded us, wagging and shivering with excitement. The night was clear and cold; the leaves on the ridge would be turning soon, first individual trees bursting into orange and then the whole huge wall of the hollow catching fire. The lights were on in my father's office and another one in my mother's bedroom, but otherwise everything was still and dark. Sarah and I stood in the middle of the barnyard and looked up at the stars; even in New Hampshire the Milky Way wasn't so present.

We got our things out of the car and then headed back out to the fields and the tent. I stuck my head in the door of my father's office when we walked past, asked him how market had gone on Saturday. It was good; they'd sold a lot more celery than he thought they would. I pressed him for more details, but he didn't seem to want to prolong the conversation.

"Is there something else wrong?"

"Everything's fine."

"Did something happen?"

There was a pause.

"The blight got to the third generation."

This generation had been planted on the hilltop, as far from the first two as possible. There was no way to know if the measures we'd taken were working—if the copper had been doing its job and killing the fungus, if burning the diseased generations and taking care not to carry the spores from one field to another were effective—but they'd been embraced enthusiastically. It was particularly hard then for everyone to realize that they'd likely been wasting their time. Nothing was safe now; my father didn't mention it, but we both knew that the fourth generation was planted on the same hilltop.

Sarah was already ahead of me, waiting in the dark, so I said good night to my father. He didn't look up from his papers, just replied, "Sleep tight," and then I said, "See you in the morning light," and he finished the little litany that I had been reciting with my parents for my entire life: "I love you." I let the spring pull the screen door shut and headed down the hill.

8

A few nights after we'd gotten home I was sitting in the field above the tent with two beers. Sarah was below me, asleep with the light on, and the tent made a faint glow in the leaves of the walnut trees above it. I heard Sarah wake up and come outside to pee; then the light clicked off, and the night went completely black. I'd made a little nest in the meadow, and I lay on my back inside it, looking up at the stars above the tips of the grass. A car passed along the top of the ridge, and I watched the headlights come along slowly and through some trick of the acoustics, I could hear the tires on the dirt road.

I stood up to go to bed, and as I gathered my things I looked back toward the barn. There was a bobbing light coming down the hill behind the barn, someone walking with a lantern. I watched it to see where it was going, and then it turned and started to come out over the humps of the fields toward me. I knew that the other apprentices were asleep; I'd seen the lights in their cabins go off. I had no idea who it might be. I sat back down and watched it come. When the light was only a hundred yards away, I called out, "Hello?" My father's voice came back, "Arlo?" He left the road and came through the high grass toward me.

"What are you doing out here?"

"Walking," he said.

"Why, what's wrong?"

"The tomatoes," he said. "The goddamn tomatoes."

There was a long pause. My father looked down into the grass and then up at the sky, then back down into the grass.

"That blight," he said finally. "It's going to kill them all. All of them."

I knew that he was being dramatic by wandering out in the dark, but I also knew that it was a real crisis. I listened to my father as he went on about the disaster, and I tried not to be impatient. He said the whole season would be a loss, that there wouldn't be enough work and the apprentices would leave. He talked about how stupid he'd been: he knew he should have destroyed the first generation of tomatoes the moment that they found the blight, and that this was his only chance at containing it. He shouldn't have hired so many people and assumed that there would be enough for everyone to do. He shouldn't have been so sure that the weather would stay dry and that the spores wouldn't be able to spread. He shouldn't have counted on the fact that he'd been growing tomatoes for forty years and that he'd somehow always made it work out in the past. He'd miscalculated, made mistakes, missed chances. And worst of all, he'd been too optimistic.

In the past, when there were other crises at the farm—a huge flood during my sophomore year in college or the major drought the second year I lived in Manhattan—I'd just heard about it on the phone. Now I was home and whether I liked it or not I was a part of this particular cataclysm. I'd tried to insulate myself by building the platform out over the hill and living far from the house, but when my father came out and found me in the dark there was nowhere else to go.

✳

The next morning the meeting in the barnyard was completely quiet. The tomato manager was in my father's office, and everyone knew that he was telling my father that the blight was in the fourth and final patch. My father came out and everyone watched him without looking at him directly. He didn't look up, just kept reading his notes, and then after a few seconds he asked if anyone wanted to start. No one said a word.

"Well," my father said. He stopped and waited. "I'm not sure what we can do next."

There was another long pause, and then he looked up. His neck was tense, his jaw tight. When he spoke again, he spit the words out.

"Just burn them all down," he said.

He went back to his office.

That was it. The tomatoes had been worth tens of thousands of dollars, money that had looked like a sure thing a

month ago. Now there was nothing to salvage, no silver lin-
ing, no learning experience. Everyone drifted away from the
shed off to other jobs, and the apprentice who was managing
the tomatoes went and got the propane torch. He turned
on the gas to test it and used a flint to spark the flame. It
burned hot and clear, nothing visible except a violent distur-
bance in the air at the torch's mouth. He pointed it toward a
patch of weeds growing in the gravel, and they wilted, curled
into themselves, went black.

Things were going to be uncomfortable for the next
few weeks. I dreaded the silent suppers at the kitchen table,
the times when my father would explode over some small
problem, the nights when he wouldn't come in from his office
until after midnight. When I'd left Massachusetts three
months before, I'd been worried that I wasn't taking enough
risks or dealing with any real consequences, and now I'd just
seen a man lose a hundred thousand dollars.

✳

The drama of the morning meeting dissipated by lunch, and
in the early afternoon my father was out of his office and
helping one of the apprentices adjust a seeder. Even if we'd
wanted to, there wasn't any time to dwell on the tomatoes;
the next morning was Saturday, and we had to get ready for
market. Everyone rushed around all afternoon building pallets in the cooler, and now, since it was the highest part of the
season, they were stacked to the ceiling with only narrow paths
between. Someone made a late delivery of blueberries, and
another person dropped off flowers. Around six o'clock my

father made a last check of everything, added a few things, and went inside to eat dinner.

At seven he sat down to eat, while it was still bright out, and then he headed upstairs to get ready for bed. I went upstairs to bring him the phone when a customer called about a special order of peaches, and he cracked the bathroom door open to accept it. The steam rolled out, smelling like soap and toothpaste, and I could see him standing at the sink. He'd always shaved without shaving cream, just held a steaming towel against his face to scald the bristles and make them soft, and his skin was bright red and scraped looking. A half hour later, at eight, still just dusk, I could hear his bedroom door close as he went to bed.

After dinner Sarah and I went down to the tent and got into bed. It was nine thirty by now, and it had just gotten dark; as we walked, there were still swallows in the dark sky and Mars was a bright star. We read for a while and turned off the light, but I couldn't fall asleep, anxious about the next morning. I'd been going to market nearly every week, but it always felt like a serious event. All the slow work in the fields, the hoeing and the harvesting, culminated in a few hours of frenzied selling. I lay awake, tossed in my sleeping bag, and eventually I drifted off.

*

The alarm went off at three o'clock. Sarah and I climbed out of our sleeping bags and got dressed in the dark, holding onto one another for support while we pulled on our pants. One of the dogs had come down with us, and she got up and stood around awkwardly, not sure why we were so busy in the middle of the night. We headed up the hill and toward the barnyard. It was crisp and completely clear, and the walnut trees in the field above the road stood out sharply. We could see our breath, and Sarah had her shoulders up around her ears, rubbing her hands together as we hurried through the wet grass.

The packing shed was all lit up when we came into the barnyard, but the other buildings around were dark, and the yard light hadn't been turned on. I could see the shadow of someone hurrying toward the summer kitchen, an apprentice going to brush her teeth. There were noises coming from the shed: the creak of the pallet jack, the heavy thump of the cooler door, the loud rolling of the pallets on the floor of the truck. Suddenly there was a crack of broken wood as a pallet was forced into place, followed by a series of crashing noises. I went up and saw my father throwing boxes of lettuce out of the truck.

His anger wasn't normal; there was something frantic about it, slightly unhinged. He saw me and yelled, "This is all wrong! Everything is completely fucked up! Whoever put these pallets together completely fucked up. They won't fit. There's no way it's going to fit!"

I started to pick up some of the boxes that he'd thrown.

"The beans are missing! I know those Jades aren't here, they can't be."

This anger was a fever that fed on itself, a cycle of recrimination and regret. The farm, the place that he had given everything to, had betrayed him. If he didn't have complete control over those acres, over those fields of tomatoes, over the boxes of lettuce that he was trying to cram into the back of the truck now, then what could he control?

I thought now, not for the first time, that he might have a heart attack there on the concrete floor of the packing shed. What would I do if he suddenly collapsed? I would run to the phone down in his office, wake up the sleepy volunteer who manned the fire station in Three Springs. I would wait while he roused another EMT and they drove the ten miles to our house. Then I would wait while they took him to the hospital in McConnellsburg, forty minutes from the farm, the red flashing lights bouncing across the empty fields, and then I would sit outside in the bright light of the inadequate emergency room.

I managed the delicate process of bringing him back to reason. I kept working, agreed with him about the mistakes, and I asked him questions that would draw the focus away from the beans. After a few minutes two apprentices came into the shed, still bleary eyed. My father had calmed down almost completely by then, and the earlier scene didn't seem like such a big deal; they helped him put the pallet back together, and one of them promised that he'd seen the beans go on the night before, so they had to be there now. The apprentices reassured him and stayed out of his way, and eventually he put the last pallet on the truck. It slid into place smoothly, filling the last square inches, and he pulled the door down roughly and latched it.

Sarah and I went to the kitchen to put coffee in our thermos, and thirty seconds later we heard one truck start and then another one, until there was a huge rumble in the barn-yard. The first of them, the one my father was driving, went barreling down the hill toward the mailbox and then up and out of the hollow. The next truck stopped in front of the house and we ran out and climbed in. The apprentice driving lurched into gear and set off to catch my father. There was a little bunk behind the seats. Sarah climbed back and pulled a blanket over herself. I wiped down the foggy windshield so that the driver could see, cleaned off the mirrors, and adjusted the heat. I poured two cups of coffee from the thermos, one for me and one for the driver, and sat back.

We caught up to my father at the end of the driveway. The headlights of the third truck were behind us now, and the convoy all pulled out onto the paved road at once, my father in the lead. He drove very fast, lumbering down the center, the smaller trees and weeds on the shoulder whipping in the backdraft, a little storm in our headlights. We came out of the darkness of the trees and into the open fields. My father kept out a close eye for deer, but he didn't slow down. He'd do his best to avoid a collision, but he'd also welded a special steel cage to the front of the trucks years ago, heavy enough to deflect a full-grown whitetail buck. The steel had been bent by past collisions, but it had always held, and on Monday, after market, someone could simply rinse it off with a hose if need be.

When we got to the end of the Boy Scout Road, my father stopped at the stop sign and the other truck idled behind him. Sarah sat up, sleepy and rumpled.

"What's going on?"

"He's eating his pie."

She grunted and lay back down. My father always put an extra pie in the cab of his truck the night before, and he always stopped and ate a little bit of it once we'd cleared the Boy Scout Road. After a minute or two the brake lights flashed, and then he was out on the smoother, larger road, accelerating. Our truck jumped and pulled out, the one behind us came too, and we were all on our way, toward Washington.

＊

The drive was 120 miles, and an hour from the city, just over South Mountain, the sky started to lighten. Here it was still farms and fields and looked probably much like it had when Confederate troops had marched through on the way to Gettysburg, misty hills and split rail fences. A few miles later, down the mountain and closer to Frederick, all the open space was filled with subdivisions and shopping centers, the road expanded to five lanes and then six, and then we were on the Beltway, driving into the city. The neighborhoods were quiet; the streetlights were still on. We passed a man in a hooded sweatshirt, a cup of coffee in one hand and the leash of his dog in the other. The dog turned his head toward the commotion of the trucks, and he and his master watched, slightly befuddled, as our battalion rolled into their quiet neighborhood and disappeared around a corner.

We stopped at the gas station on River Road, and the clerk handed over the bathroom key just as he'd been doing for fifteen years. We washed our faces in the sink, and someone brushed his teeth; then we gathered again in the parking lot. My father was already back in his truck and had started it, but the rest of us paused to pour cups of coffee from the thermos. We stretched our legs, talked about how hot it was going to get, and put off getting back into the trucks for as long as we could.

We pulled into the school yard at seven. My father parked the truck, coming in way too fast and then stopping exactly where he wanted to, his bumper just a few inches from the wall of the building that sat beside the lot where we were going to set up. He opened the back door, raising it just a few inches against some unexpected resistance, and the cold air we'd brought with us from the coolers at the farm flowed out. A few raspberries also rolled out of the gap, and we watched as they landed on the bumper. My father threw the door up all at once, and there were raspberries spilled everywhere; a few flats had collapsed, leaning drunkenly against the door, and they came pouring out, rolling across the pavement.

There wasn't time to dwell on the loss. The doors of the other trucks rolled up noisily, and an apprentice jumped into the back of each one and started handing down boxes to everyone still standing at the back. Eight or nine local kids also helped at these markets, mostly high school kids, and everyone ran the boxes out into the open space, set them down, and came back for more. We worked quickly, my father's constant patter in the background, "Let's go everybody; we're late, we're late. Put that bread over there; the eggs go here beside the tree. We need more lettuce out here. Fix these mushroom boxes and get the tables up for the flowers."

After an hour, there were three lines of vegetables set up, maybe fifty feet long, with aisles between them so that people could shop. There were two tables of herbs and another one of flowers. There was a set of tall wicker baskets filled with loaves of different breads, and a table filled with pies, cookies, and pastries. There were coolers of cheese and eggs, and one of frozen chickens. There was a huge arrangement of berries, flats of plums, and baskets of peaches. There were flat cases of lettuce, bunches of chard, a mountain of beets. I stopped and looked at it for a second, all spread out there in the bright sun, waiting.

A few customers always came early and hung around watching. A man stuck his head in the back of the truck to ask if there were going to be any Nittany apples, but the guy unloading didn't stop moving boxes, just paused for a second to make it clear that he was bothered. "Yeah, we've got them in here. We open at eight." The man said thanks and reported back to the group of other customers, then returned to his car to sit alone and listen to the radio.

At eight, the cashiers threw their boxes open, and a line of customers formed. They brought up baskets of raspberries and bags of lettuce and piled it all on the table. The cashiers weighed everything, tallied the prices on calculators, and the line started to move. The customers handed over cash or wrote checks, and the cashiers made change. Then they bagged everything up and handed it over. The customers struggled off to their cars, lugging heavy canvas LL Bean bags they brought with them or the paper bags we provided, and another customer moved up and took a place at the table.

I was cashiering at the end of the table, and I didn't look up again for the first hour. By eight fifteen the line already had fifty people in it, and it was getting longer, and the crowd still shopping was another hundred people. The orders were huge, sometimes three or four shopping baskets full of vegetables. I weighed four pounds of okra and two pounds of crimini mushrooms, counted three loaves of multigrain bread and two sourdough baguettes, bagged up three pints of blueberries and two quarts of apricots. I weighed chickens and blocks of yogurt cheese, bunches of dill and parsley, boxes of small red potatoes. I told the customer the total, sometimes more than a hundred dollars' worth of vegetables, and they handed it over gladly.

The only time I stopped was when my father found out that he'd been right: the green beans weren't all there. He got on the phone and called home. My mother reported that there were seven cases of them sitting on the other loading dock. He looked at his watch and made the calculation about when they'd get there, looked over at the quickly emptying cases of the beans we hadn't forgotten. "I think we need them." There was a pause while my mother argued. "Just send him, we need them. And tell him to drive fast."

※

By ten thirty my father was selling vegetables as fast as he could. He went around and opened new boxes of peas, heaped up the display of lettuce, directed the apprentices to get more bread or to consolidate the baskets of peaches. While he did this, he was talking to a constant stream of customers, telling someone how to cook something, someone else how much longer we'd have nectarines, someone else a price. A scrum of middle-aged women had developed around him, three or four of them waiting to ask him some question or another, and the woman he was talking to had her hand on his arm and was laughing at some joke he'd just made. I went over to ask him a question from a customer about how much longer we'd have blueberries, and I had to wait in line like everyone else.

By the time I got his attention a man holding a little boy was talking to him, and the little boy was smiling shyly. "Jim's a farmer, Noah!" The boy looked at him and smiled again, then looked away. "He loves the raspberries," the man said to my father, and he nodded gladly. "They are beautiful right now," my father said. He smiled at the kid. "I remember you from when you were just a baby! How old are you now, four?" The boy looked away. My father asked him if he wanted to get up on the back of the truck. He couldn't resist the offer and beamed while my father picked him up and set him down next to a stack of cabbage boxes.

My father left the boy and his father on the back of the truck and walked toward a pile of corn and picked up an ear. He opened it, looked at the kernels, and had a bite. Without looking up, he yelled, "Folks, we've got beautiful corn today! Really beautiful! It came out of the field yesterday morning, folks, and it's fresh as can be. We're so proud of this corn." Two or three people came over while he walked away to check on the carrots. Within a minute there were ten people around the corn, squeezing the ears and filling up bags of it. A woman said to a stranger next to her, "He says it was picked yesterday," as they both grabbed another ear.

"Folks, if you haven't tried kohlrabi, you need to give it a chance. It's right over here; we've got a great crop." A woman picked up one of the weird green bulbs and looked at it suspiciously. "How do you eat this?" "Well, just peel it and slice it thinly, put a little salt on it. I eat it almost every day." It was salesmanship but it was also the truth. "How do you pick them out?" the woman asked. "Well, they're all good, really. These are two nice ones," he said and handed them to her. She put them in her bag. He turned away, still talking. "Folks," he said, "we've got some great green beans this week. They're called Jade, and they're some of the best we grow."

Over the years, my father had developed relationships with hundreds of people at his market. Some of them had been buying vegetables from him for forty years, and he knew their sons and daughters, and often their grandkids too. Some of the conversations were just about how well the apricots had worked in a tart the week before or about how much basil was needed to make a cup of pesto, but some were more serious. At one point he stepped away and spoke quietly with a woman whose husband was sick, and later a very old man found him and pulled him aside to talk about the problems he'd been having with his hip. He spent time with each person, patiently, and he also worked while they talked, adjusting a display of leeks or picking out a few bad raspberries.

Lots of these customers knew me and my sister too, and when they came up to the table to have their purchases rung

up, they asked me about how I'd liked living in Massachusetts, about Sarah, about how my sister was doing and if she
liked living in Pittsburgh. Sometimes some of the older ones,
women especially, would ask me what my plans were, if I was
going to get married soon and if I had a good plan for finding
work after the season was over, and sometimes they gave unsolicited advice about how I should go about finding an apartment, or demanded that I e-mail someone they knew who
might have a lead on a good job.

During the first two decades that my father set up markets in
these neighborhoods, he had always alerted his customers that
he was there by holding a bell out the window of the truck and
hitting it with a wrench as he drove slowly along. There were a
few other simple marketing techniques; on days in January
when the weather was horrible, he handed out "corn coupons,"
which entitled people to three free ears of corn when they
came back in August, and every spring he mailed out a sched-
ule of markets to a mailing list he kept in an old manila folder.

His relationships were the most important part of marketing
his business. The co-op handled most of the wholesale business,
to chefs and stores, and so almost all of my father's customers
were people from the neighborhood. Most people walked to
market, but some of them drove, and they often owned old
Volvos or Mercedes with stickers in the back window from
Princeton and Grinnell College. It was a crowd typical of the
neighborhoods in Washington where he'd always set up, Cleveland Park and the Palisades. They generally leaned liberal, and
many of them worked somehow with the government.

There was a general counsel for the congressional Republicans, along with the directors of organizations that covered food safety and another who handled consumer protection. There were hundreds of lawyers, and just as many mid-level bureaucrats, and there were ambassadors and journalists. A curator of Dutch painting from the National Gallery came, and a woman who had worked at *National Geographic* for forty years. My father knew some of these people very well, and even occasionally socialized with some of them outside of market, but he was extremely proud of all his customers.

At eleven, the green pickup from the farm pulled up with the missing beans. My father ran down to the truck and started to pull the boxes from the back, ran them up, and set them in the empty space.

"Folks, everyone should know that the beans just got here. We love these beans, folks, really love them; they're called Jade, and they're some of the best ones we grow."

A few people came over and started to pick up handfuls.

"Really, folks, you can trust me about these beans. They're a great size right now, and this is the peak of the season for them."

Now there was a small knot of people filling bags, a slight frenzy around the boxes.

"I'm serious, folks, these beans really are delicious. I ate them for dinner last night with just a little butter, and that was all they needed."

Half of the box was gone in a minute or two, and my father opened up another one. He set it to the side and stood back, watching people take his good advice, and then he moved on to the snap peas.

It was hot by now, the grubby heat that Washington was known for, and everyone was sweating. There were frozen jugs of water in the coolers with the cheese, and every few minutes someone checked them to see if they had melted into water they could drink. There were ten cashiers working now, all full tilt, and when someone left to use the bathroom, the line in front of the tables swelled noticeably. A cashier's calculator stopped working, so she tallied the orders on a paper bag while she waited for a replacement. Another cashier tried to eat a pear and had to set it down after a single bite, abandoning it to the yellow jackets while she helped the next customer.

The people stocking the vegetables never stopped either. They ran a constant circuit, taking out full boxes and coming back with a stack of empties in their arms, reporting back to the people in the trucks which supplies were getting low. An apprentice with a fifty-pound box of watermelons in his hands shouldered his way through the crowd, and another person tried to empty a few new sacks of corn onto the pile. The customers couldn't wait and grabbed the new ears directly out of the bag—he had to gently nudge them away, like kittens at a bowl of milk. The crowd had been this steady for four hours, and there were no signs of it slowing down.

*

By twelve thirty my father was complaining about how we hadn't brought enough.

"We had four more cases of eggplant in the cooler! I can't believe we left it. And all that basil too, it's just going to go to waste. We did sell a lot of broccoli though. Holy shit, we brought a lot. It really was beautiful. And thank god we got those beans. That was three hundred dollars we'd have missed!"

By one o'clock almost everything was gone; a man with a stroller and a tennis racket was shuffling through the last five or six rutabagas in the bottom of a box, and a woman wearing a faded T-shirt that announced her support for the '88 Dukakis/Bentsen ticket filled up a bag with three cracked kohlrabi. A woman in a ratty hand-knit sweater, a person that the cashiers were all familiar with, showed up right at closing and tried to bargain for any bruised vegetables we had left over, offering three dollars for a box of cantaloupes. Eventually she got them and piled them in the backseat of her old Corolla.

The crew went around and closed up what was left, carried everything back to the truck, and handed it up. The remainder of the sixteen full pallets we'd brought that morning, stacked eight feet high, now made just one little pile.

The crew stood around while my father counted out the money he owed to the local kids, counting out twenties from the piles in the bottom of the cash boxes, putting them in envelopes and handing them over. Everyone was exhausted, and we sat on the curb and drank a jug of water in the heat, eager to get in the trucks and get out of there. Just as the last envelope was being handed over, a blue Volvo pulled into the lot and a woman jumped out.

"Are you guys all closed up?"

My father had been climbing up into the driver's seat but now he got back down.

"What are you looking for?"

"I don't know, maybe some lettuce?"

He shook his head. "All gone."

"A tomato?"

"We have some squash and some basil, and I think there's a pie, maybe apple."

"OK," she said, "I'll take that."

One of the apprentices got out of the truck and opened up the back door. He climbed into the dark and started moving things around, handing down the boxes that were in the way, unpacking enough to get down to the pies. He found one and handed it out. "All I have is a hundred-dollar bill," the woman said. My father dug through to the cash boxes, made her change, and thanked her. As she got in her car, another person pulled up. He rolled down his window. "Do you have any pies left?" My father got down again and went around back.

Eventually we pulled away from the school yard and went to eat lunch at a cheap Thai place on Connecticut Avenue. Everyone was dirty and sweaty, and they gave us a big table in the back and brought beers while we looked at the menu. We ate our pad thai and spring rolls and drank our beers. By now, once my father washed his hands and sat down and had half a beer in him, he was heady with excitement. "What a day!" he said. "What a day! Can you believe we sold all those Jades? I couldn't believe it. Those things are beautiful. I ate them last night for dinner and they were absolutely perfect."

Everyone was tired, but they were happy to sit quietly and listen to him talk, and to rest.

"I swear, we could sell twice as much stuff! Sometimes I just think we could sell twice as much! People just love this stuff, they love it!" He seemed surprised, even after doing the same thing for all these years, that he could still bring vegetables to the city, set them out on the pavement, and sell them all.

When we left the restaurant, the crew of apprentices split up into the three trucks to go home. Sarah went in a different truck so that she'd have room to lie down, but I rode with my dad. By the time we were back on the Beltway, *A Prairie Home Companion* had come on the radio; no one in our family had ever been a big fan of Garrison Keillor, but it was the program on WAMU at that hour, so we were stuck with it. As I sat there I considered how many times in my life I had done this drive with my father or my mother. I'd been coming to Washington with them for thirty years, hours that added up to days and weeks, tucked into a narrow bed, with my father humming to himself. I drifted off, and when I woke up he was playing his harmonica to keep himself awake, "Amazing Grace" and "Oh! Susanna" in reedy notes.

After an hour my father got off an exit and went to McDonald's. He went inside and bought a black coffee and a small Coke. Then he parked the truck at the very back of the lot, put the brake on, climbed down, walked over to a small patch of grass where a few cherry trees grew, and lay down in their shade. After a minute his chest was rising and falling evenly, and I could hear him snoring. I sat in the cab and read, then went inside to use the bathroom. After a while he stirred and sat up, rubbed his eyes, and got back in the truck. He drank some of his coffee, and we pulled back out onto the highway.

That night, after he'd unloaded the truck and spent a few hours in his office, he came inside and sat at the kitchen table to relax. The next day, Sunday, when my mother would go to Washington to sell at the farmers' market at Dupont Circle, he'd get up a little late, make coffee, and drive to the gas station in Three Springs to pick up the special-ordered copy of the *New York Times* they saved for him. He'd have a late breakfast of eggs and toast, listen to the radio, linger over a cup of coffee. In the afternoon he'd go out to his office for a few hours, but he wouldn't work too hard, just putter around and deal with loose ends. He'd be in for dinner, and then he'd go to bed late, and in the morning he'd wake up and start the week.

✳

If I worried about my father, I also understood why he was so completely consumed by his work. I wanted him to be calm all the time, to never lose his temper, but it made me glad to see him sell all those vegetables, and to get so much satisfaction out of putting another bunch of radishes in someone's basket. This was his life, not mine, and it wasn't my place to tell him that he shouldn't care so much about a missing box of beans.

Eventually, after a few more weeks, the crisis with the tomatoes was almost completely forgotten. It wasn't the first time something like this had happened, a significant loss that couldn't be recovered. There had been years when the farm made almost no money at all and years when it had been flush. In 1976 the loss of just a hundred dollars might have required an uncomfortable conversation with the bank at the end of the month, but my parents weren't living hand to mouth any more. They weren't rich, not by any stretch, but the business was strong enough now that it wasn't in constant danger of being snuffed out. The farm would tend to itself in one way or another.

9

A few weeks later the mornings were cold and things were winding down everywhere on the farm. We all bundled up at the morning meetings in old flannel shirts and padded overalls, taking off layers as the day warmed up. The frost hadn't come yet, but everyone was looking forward to it. Afterward we wouldn't need to pick the basil anymore, or the squash, and the work would move toward cleaning up: collecting the tomato stakes out of the fields, catching up on carpentry projects, hours inside with a propane heater trimming bins of celeriac.

Sarah and I woke up early to pick the last of the season's corn, and we rode down on the wagon with four others. An apprentice climbed into a big wooden bin used to collect the corn, and he nestled into the empty sacks in the bottom to fall asleep as the wagon jostled along. When the tractor stopped, he pulled his wool hat off his eyes, stretched, and jumped down, landing heavily in his boots. The fog lay over the field, and only the first twenty feet or so of the rows were visible. It was cold, and the stalks were silver in the dew, and the trees stood up sternly at the edges of the field. It was quiet except for the sound of the creek, too early for the birds.

We moved into the corn, and it swallowed us completely; soon I was all alone in my section of the patch. I moved down the high walls of the row, squeezing each ear to feel the kernels beneath the husk to make sure it was ripe, and then I snapped the ones that were ready off the stalks. They made a satisfying crack, like breaking a small bone. I put three dozen ears in the first bag, and when it was full, I left it to be collected after the picking was done. Then I got another bag out and started to fill it, moving slowly through the mist.

Eventually I got to the end of my row and came out into the open again. I took off the raincoat I'd been wearing to protect myself from the dew, let it air out, and then I went back into the field. Now I was picking from the other end, moving to meet the person coming toward me. After a few minutes I could see a little rustle in the distance, and then I saw Sarah. She was squeezing each ear, testing it, and filling her own bag. She had on a raincoat and pants that were too big for her, and she'd rolled up the sleeves and the cuffs. She looked up and saw me, and we both smiled.

When all the rows were finished, the tractor drove directly down the center of the field, crushing the stalks and leaving a wide avenue behind it, a feeling of the seas being parted. This was the last time this patch would be picked, so there was no reason not to run it down. We passed one of the fields of tomatoes on the way back up to the barnyard. The plants were all dead, brown and stiff in their rusty cages, and nobody gave them a second look. The landscape had been light green just a few months ago, the sun glowing in the new leaves, the ground damp and soft. Now everything was more rigid, the leaves stiff and about to fall, the dirt of the road packed and hard. There was a smell of burning in the air, smoke from a nearby brush fire.

✳

That afternoon was quiet, so I decided that I would drive up to the county seat and see what I could find in the records there about Bert's murder. After seeing Blue Moon again and visiting with Chloe, I was curious to see if there were any primary sources about the events of that day. The courthouse was a big building in the middle of town, built in a style common to central Pennsylvania, with a domed belfry I could see from a distance. The parking lot was almost empty. It was cool inside, dimly lit, and it smelled like an old elementary school. The floors were black-and-white checkerboard, there was heavy woodwork around the doors and windowsills, and the ceilings were high. The only person around was a deputy sitting by the metal detector.

He directed me toward a long hall with frosted doors every few feet. The lights were off in all the offices I passed, and I didn't stop to look at the dark glass cases of historical artifacts. At the end of the hall I came to a door with black lettering that identified it as the Office of the County Clerk. There was a faint yellow glow behind the glass, and I wasn't sure if I should knock. I tried the knob and it turned, so I opened the door and stepped inside. Four women all looked up at once. I took off my hat and approached the counter, and the sound of typing resumed. The receptionist had on a dress and stockings, a tight hairdo, and she had a lazy eye.

"Can I help you with something?"

"I'm looking for some records about a case from nineteen ninety."

"What sort of a case was it?"

"A murder."

I was glad that I hadn't changed after work, that I was still a little muddy from digging potatoes that morning. I didn't look exactly like I was a local, but it was probably close enough. The woman slid over a ledger book, oversized and with a marbled cover.

"It'll be in here. Just look up the case number, and I can go down in the basement and get the records."

I opened the book, ran my finger down the list of handwritten entries, until I found the approximate dates I was looking for. George William Robb was there. She wrote a number down on a scrap of paper and left the room. She came back and put a thin folder on the counter.

"This is everything we have here. I don't know if there might be more somewhere else, maybe at the state police barracks. Anything else you'll be needing?"

I didn't really know anything about Robb except that he was an old man. I didn't know anything about the other witness, or what had been said during the confrontation, or what had happened after Bert was shot, but the whole story was here in this folder of fifty-four typewritten pages, bound in manila that smelled of storage. They provided a concise explanation of the crime. I was probably the first person to request these documents since a few months after Bert's death, and twenty years later it was likely that I'd be the last.

There was a very short list of those present at the crime scene: Robb, Bert, Lina, two apprentices, Sally White and Robert Weinswig, and a local woman referred to only as Diana. Robert Weinswig provided most of the information because the main document was a transcript of his appearance in court during a preliminary investigation of the crime. The only other witness called was the doctor who had performed the autopsy. I was surprised to see my father's name on the eighth page of the document, but it was just incidental; when the judge asked Robert how he'd originally heard of the job at Blue Moon, he answered that Jim Crawford had referred him.

※

Later that afternoon, after I left the courthouse, I went to the public library a few blocks away to try to find a picture of Robb in the newspaper archive by scrolling through the microfiche. There wasn't much at all about the murder, just one paragraph printed the day after it happened. Locals wouldn't need a picture to know what Bill Robb looked like because he'd been the mailman in the area for decades. He was also familiar enough that his personal problems were public knowledge. A motion filed after the murder listed a few reasons why a local jury might be prejudiced against Robb. The last one was the shortest: "Among many residents of Huntingdon County, Mr. Robb has a reputation of being a 'drunk.'"

On a form that Robb had filled out about his assets, he listed his home and a '79 Pontiac. He wrote that he had no outstanding loans, and in answer to the question "Do you have any money?" he had just written "No." On another form he'd written his full name ("GEORGE WILLIAM ROBB"), his age ("69"), how far he'd gone in school ("HIGH SCHOOL GRADUATE Approx. 3 yrs. College"), if he understood the English language ("YES"), and then, in answer to the question "Have you ever been a patient in a mental institution?" ("YES"). Around 1964, he wasn't sure of the exact date, he'd been hospitalized at Mercer Hospital. ("ALCOHOLISM AND STRESS.")

Robb's handwriting was spidery with tremors, but it was aggressively capitalized. Knowing his profession and his reputation for drunkenness, I imagined him as a stock character, the anonymous postal worker with a desperate secret. I saw him in a suit of blue polyester, short-sleeved dress shirt, stiff pants, and heavy black shoes, a gray stubble on the cheeks, a permanent shuffle in his gait, bags under his eyes that sagged a little and showed the red beneath the lids. I imagined that his job involved weekday hangovers, fluorescent lighting, gray rooms full of mail carts that rolled like gurneys with bad wheels.

Robb's actual words were only transcribed a few times in the documents. Mostly they were responses to questions from the judge, technicalities about whether or not he understood certain proceedings, and usually only requiring an answer of yes or no. A few times the judge deviated from the standard script and asked Robb questions about his health. He asked if he was taking any medications, and Robb responded that he had a prescription for "nerve pills." When he was asked about his mental state, Robb responded, "Excellent," and when he was asked if he had any questions for the judge before he was declared guilty, Robb said, "Let's get this terminated."

The only time Robb said more than a few words that were transcribed by the court was to express a complaint about a letter he mailed to the Pennsylvania attorney general that was never answered. It had been directed elsewhere without his permission, and he claimed that that act was an infringement on his constitutional rights. The judge, the district attorney, and the defense attorney all said that they'd read Robb's letter, that he shouldn't have expected it to be private, that the contents of the letter were pointless anyway, and that the Constitution didn't have anything to do with it.

In short, there just wasn't much documentation available about Robb's life or about the kind of person he was. When I looked in the archives of the *Daily News*, there were only four mentions of Robb in the sixty-nine years he'd lived in Huntingdon County. The first detailed how he had been hit by a car when he was a little boy after he "ran into the street directly in front of an automobile" in 1927. The second reported the deep lacerations his daughter had suffered on her skull when she fell out of a car on the way to church on a Sunday morning in 1949. The third was the paragraph-long report about Bert's murder, and the fourth was Robb's obituary. It was short.

⁜

According to Robert Weinswig's account, he had spent the morning of May 2, 1990, working on potatoes with Sally and Diana, getting them ready for planting by cutting out the eyes. At eleven o'clock they were finishing up and loading bushel baskets into the back of a pickup when they saw a car pull up the dirt road. It stopped and Diana went over to talk to the driver, whom they all recognized as Robb. She'd been working on the farm for a few years, and she knew the neighbors. Robert and Sally had only been there for a few weeks. Robert had just graduated with a degree in arts education and moved that spring from Ann Arbor, Michigan; Sally had come to the farm from Boston.

Robb started yelling at Diana, loud enough that everyone in the field could hear what he had to say. He was slurring his words and yelling about dogs, that Bert's dogs were bothering his horse. He yelled about his responsibilities and his rights as a landowner and threw Diana a book, the Pennsylvania game warden's manual. Robb started to talk about his military service and how Bert had done everything he could to avoid serving. He knew all about Bert, how he was a radical and an agitator, that he was an outsider without enough common courtesy to keep his dogs away from a man's horse.

He repeated his points over and over, and he smelled like liquor. When he was finished talking he pulled the car away. He stopped ten feet farther on and called back to them, announcing that he was giving Bert two days to respond to his complaints about his dogs. He was being reasonable, giving Bert a chance to do the right thing and fix the problem. It was a simple issue, just a matter of neighborliness, and he wasn't asking too much. If Bert didn't fix the problem, Robb might take matters into his own hands and shoot the dogs himself. He drove on some more, but then he stopped again. He yelled his full name out the window and across the fields: "George William Robb."

Complaints about dogs are familiar in the country. My parents' dogs had caused problems too: harassing cows, nearly killing a neighbor's terrier, roaming around producing unwanted puppies. Our dog Peanut barked constantly at the hunters who walked along the wall of the ridge above our house, scaring away the deer, and when I was fourteen I'd found her huddled under the front porch, whining and refusing to come out. When we finally dragged her free, I saw that she had been shot in her flank, a perfect piercing of a single round fired from a deer rifle when someone had finally lost his temper.

Robert mentioned four dogs in the transcript, but I remembered only two in particular, Sailor and Moon. They were long and sleek, with sharp muzzles, bright eyes, and a careful, refined, almost delicate manner. After Robb drove away, Robert asked Diana if he would really shoot the dogs. It must have seemed strange to someone who had just moved from Ann Arbor that a neighbor would threaten violence like that. Diana, who knew how these things turned out sometimes, just said, "I don't know."

❋

Diana was gone when Robb came back that afternoon, but now there were four people in the field along the road planting squash: Robert and Sally again, but now Lina too, and Bert himself. It was five thirty in the afternoon, and the sun was still bright, but it must have been shady in the valley and getting cold. The birds would have stopped calling by then, and it would have been quiet. They'd just finished getting the last of the squash into the ground and were watering it in. Bert was apart from the others because he was still planting, finding room for a few more.

They heard Robb's car before they saw it. He pulled up slowly and rolled down his window. He asked Robert if he'd given Bert his message. Robert ignored him because Bert was just ten feet away, and he could hear the conversation himself. The dogs were barking now, riled up, and someone told them to stop and to be quiet. Bert ignored Robb and tried to keep working. Robert testified that Robb was just saying "the same old stuff," and that it wasn't an argument as much as a barely coherent summary of the grievances he'd already laid out that morning.

If this had only been an argument about the dogs, it might have ended then. Robb would have said his piece and driven home. It was clear almost immediately though that the dogs weren't the real problem. Robb looked at Bert down in the field, still planting squash and trying to keep busy.

"You don't respect me," Robb said. "You don't respect anyone."

Bert couldn't ignore this; it was an accusation almost perfectly calculated to make him respond, an appeal to his first principles.

"That's not true," Bert said. "I do respect you."

Here was Bert, out in the field on a beautiful day in early May, planting squash seedlings with his wife, on a farm they were building up together. His daughter was in the yard behind the barn, playing in the grass while her grandmother hung clean laundry. He wasn't bothering anybody or causing any trouble. All he was doing was trying to grow vegetables for a living, completely dedicated to his own work and too busy to be bothering anybody else.

It probably couldn't have occurred to Bert that there was nothing he could say that would have satisfied Robb. Bert had spent all his life so far making arguments about justice, being led away by police after protesting for someone else's rights, leading presidential campaigns dedicated to the idea that everyone deserved a fair shake. He'd come to Pennsylvania because he wanted to put those ideals into action and live a life that was productive and respectful, that didn't cause any harm and might make the world a better place. Any logical person could see that he was doing everything right. It couldn't have occurred to Bert that Robb might just hate him.

This murder might have been about the divide between rural people and those who live in the city, between locals and outsiders. It could have been about the way of life in Appalachia, or Pennsylvania, or Huntingdon County, or even just Walker Township. Maybe, worst of all, it really was just about dogs. But I don't think any of that was true. I think this was the reason it happened: Robb had nothing left to believe in, and he was jealous of the man who did. I believe that because of what Robb said after Bert had made his case about respect:

"I don't care about my life."

And Bert, standing below him on the ground that he'd tilled himself, feeling the cool breeze off the pond he'd dug, hearing the noise of his little girl playing in the barnyard, said,

"Well, I care about mine."

✳

Robb finally got out of the car. He was holding a shotgun in his hands, a Savage model 24 V A 222/20. All the people in the field stood up from where they'd been kneeling down in the dirt with their zucchini seedlings. They all turned toward Robb and started to reason with him. They asked him to put the gun away, to get back in his car and drive home, not to hurt anyone. The dogs were there too, but now Robb ignored them, forgot that they were the reason he'd come in the first place. Sally turned slowly and moved toward the bottom of the field. She hid behind a tree there, and the dogs followed her. The last time that Robert saw them, they were wagging their tails.

There was a moment before the shot when everything was still, for what seemed to Robert like ten seconds. Robb stood there and pointed the shotgun at Bert. Bert was just ten feet away and downhill, and there was no way for him to avoid whatever would happen next. Robert saw Bert's face, and he told the court, "It was just like he kind of knew." At that moment Bert did move, though it wasn't toward Robb or his wife. He turned toward his work, back to the planting, and knelt down to put another squash seedling in the ground.

Robb said one more thing before he shot Bert. The words

were awkwardly phrased but almost perfectly calculated to prove how heartless he was, and how little sympathy he deserved. He said, "I'm really sorry to have to make Chloe fatherless."

✳

Robb pulled the trigger and the scene exploded. Lina screamed at Robb, "Get out of here! Just get out of here!" Robb got back in his car and started to drive toward the barnyard, toward Chloe and the house, but then he turned around at the last minute and drove back out the road. Robert had run away and hid because he was sure that Robb was going to try and kill everyone in the field, but when he saw Lina struggling with Bert, he ran back and helped her load him into the pickup. Lina got in the driver's seat and yelled at Robert, "Run, call the hospital and tell them I'm coming," and then she raced down the road toward Huntingdon.

My sister and I were already home from school that afternoon, and I remember being out in the barnyard when my mother came out of the house and screamed that someone had shot Bert. I remember the sound of screen doors slamming, and my mother's face, and the flat light of early spring. I remember waiting that afternoon after my mother left, worried but also excited. I was twelve years old and caught up in something incredibly dramatic. I was too young to believe that Bert might really die. My father went back to his office and waited for my mother to call from the pay phone at the hospital.

When my mother got to the hospital, she found Lina in

the waiting room still wearing clothes stained with blood and dirt. Lina was calm when the doctor finally came out and told her that Bert was dead. She was exhausted, in shock. The doctor asked if she'd like to see the body, and she said that she would. She asked my mother to come with her, and they walked together into the operating room where Bert was now laid out on a metal table. She hugged him and told him that she loved him. Then she found a pair of scissors and cut off the finger of a latex glove. She cut a lock of Bert's hair and put it into the piece of glove, hugged him once more, and left.

My mother called before she left and told my father that Bert had died. It was late at night, and when she and my father were finished talking, he came to my sister's room, where we were waiting, and told us. My father sobbed and hugged us to him. It was the first time that either of us had ever seen an adult so helpless.

✻

Before he shot Bert, Robb had said that he didn't care about his life. It was dramatic, especially in context, but I understood what he was saying on some level. I had an inkling of that feeling sometimes in Cambridge, walking through the dirty snow to an office and a job that didn't give me any pleasure. It was the feeling I had when I saw all the kids in Harvard Yard so busy, so confident that they knew what they were doing, while I was just drifting along without any clear destination or sense of purpose. Sometimes, like Robb, I also got drunk enough that the sense of hopelessness would recede. I knew that depression like that could metastasize, could turn ordinary people mean, make them bitter about other people's pleasure.

Bert had probably felt this way too at some points in his life, but the difference was that he'd done something about it. He decided to make the most of his time by coming out to Pennsylvania to start a farm. My parents had done the same thing; they had planted their first crop of tomatoes forty years ago and watched them all die, had spent years enduring floods and droughts, and then had planted another crop of tomatoes just to see them die again. Any progress was slow and incremental, and sometimes it was impossible to see at all. Even so, they kept at it, believed in the farm and the vegetables it produced, kept breaking up the fields every spring because it was the way they'd chosen to give their lives purpose.

All that ambition could be hard on other people. In the police report submitted by Wayne Gibson, the officer who responded to the call of a shooting in Walker Township, he wrote that during the argument that preceded the shooting, "Mr. Robb told Mr. Deleeuw that he was selfish." That sounded like an oddly personal insult, something that lovers might say, or brothers. But I also understood the feeling. When I was little and worried about my mother's happiness, or when I desperately wanted to be in a place where there were other kids, I felt like something had been taken away from me, that there had been a trade that I hadn't had any say in. The truth was that the farm asked a lot of all of us.

But it wasn't just when I was a little kid that I felt that way. When I'd been in the packing shed before market, watching my father rage about the beans and wondering if this might be the time that it would be too much for his heart, I felt angry that I had to worry about him. When he came out to find me to tell me that the tomatoes were ruined and the season was a catastrophe, I felt resentful that he had assumed I would listen. When he sat silently at dinner and brooded about carrots, I wanted to leave the table and abandon him to eat alone. When he punished himself for the failures of the farm, he didn't seem to realize that we all had to stand around and watch.

But in being a part of lives lived with such fierce commitment I'd gained something much more important. My father once told me that he wondered if the farm had been worth it. There were so many other things he could have done with his life. I said that maybe that was true, but I was genuinely proud of what he and my mother had done. I told him I wouldn't have wanted to grow up any other way, and they were both the best example I had of how to live, and I meant every word.

✳

Before the judge dismissed Robert from the witness stand, he asked if he was going to stay and finish out the rest of the season on Blue Moon. "Yeah, I am," Robert said. Robert had only been in Pennsylvania for two weeks before Bert was murdered while he watched. He'd indicated before in the transcript that this was just a summer job, a chance to try some farming. Even so, there was something that made him feel like he needed to stay and finish what he'd started. He had signed on to something important at Blue Moon, and he was going to see it through.

Lina and Chloe stayed for one more season. Then Lina sold the farm to the doctor and the blacksmith and went to work at an organization in Kentucky whose mission was to support the revitalization of Appalachia through arts projects. She fell in love again, remarried, and had another daughter. Eventually she moved to Maine, bought the house where I'd visited Chloe, got a job that she loved, kept painting and drawing, and raised her family.

They'd been back to Blue Moon that one time, the Thanksgiving when Chloe had gone with her, and she kept the shoe box of pictures, invitations, and announcements. She also planted the garden in Maine and tended to it, a small patch of vegetables and a living reminder of her time as a farmer. I understood the sense of obligation that kept them there for the rest of that last season at Blue Moon. She wanted to continue the work that she and Bert had started together; she wanted to harvest what they'd planted.

※

A week after my trip to the courthouse I was talking to my mother about Bert, and she told me a story about how he'd once filled his hollow bamboo fishing pole with pot and smuggled it through customs on his way home from Belize. As the conversation wound down, she went to her desk and found an old copy of the *Washington Post Magazine* that featured a story about Bert and his murder. It had been published in November 1990, approximately six months after he'd died.

It was the definitive account, and the people who cared about Bert spoke clearly in the article. Lina said the most. She was angry, still struggling with the injustice of what Robb had done. Bert's friends talked about how he had pushed them to action when they were afraid and had supported and soothed them in different ways. The writer had even conducted a short interview with Bill Robb, not yet convicted but in jail awaiting resolution of his case. He was mostly incoherent. He didn't take any responsibility for his crime, justifying his anger because Bert hadn't controlled his dogs, and he ultimately blamed Bert for "walking into the shot."

✳

At the end of the hearing, the public defender asked the coroner to speak about the nature of the wound. He wanted to make a case that Robb might have shot Bert in self-defense. He had asked Robert earlier if Bert might have had a farming implement in his hand, and he wanted to know if Robb had said, "Stay where you are, leave me alone." This seemed unlikely since Robb was holding a gun on an unarmed man, but Robert said no, he never heard those words. There were a few more questions about positioning and distances, but they sounded implausible. It was hard to imagine that it was self-defense, especially considering the fact that Robb had shot Bert in the back.

The coroner was impatient; he'd been called away from the hospital and had walked down to the courthouse to testify. He described the anatomy and the shot pattern, and how a shotgun shell causes damage. He testified that the wound was inevitably fatal. He couldn't be convinced to elaborate, just gave his measurements and other observations. His only deviation from the empirical facts was when he was asked if extraordinary measures might have saved Bert. He chose not to deny the possibility of a miracle, and he closed with a statement that also might have served, in some small way, to help sum up Bert's life: "Human beings are amazing creatures."

During Robb's guilty plea, the judge couldn't help but comment on his looks: "Mr. Robb is certainly showing the ravages of his sixty-nine years, perhaps more than other folks his same age or even older." This might have been sympathy, but it also sounded like a comment on the length of the prison term he was about to hand down: ten years that were essentially a death sentence. Robb died five years after he shot Bert, in prison, as alone as he could be.

10

By the end of September the farm was thriving again. There were more than a hundred flats of raspberries coming out of the field each week and no sign of them slowing down. They had never been a major crop for the farm and hadn't gotten a lot of attention, but that spring my father had talked to a raspberry grower in upstate New York who had suggested a different method of trimming the canes in the fall. Suddenly and without warning they were producing huge amounts of fruit, four times more than they ever had before.

We had so many raspberries that there weren't enough places to sell them all. The berries were extremely perishable, lasting only a few days, and they were also expensive to pick. They were worth a lot at market though, so there was a chance to make some serious money. The co-op couldn't take them all, so my father was constantly on the phone, trying to find buyers. He'd sold a bunch of flats to a woman who made jam, and a man from Washington who owned a gelato store drove up from the city and took twenty flats once a week. We were selling them at market too, and getting a good price, but there were just too many to get rid of.

Everyone was in a better mood suddenly. The raspberry crop was giving everyone hope that the finances of the season wouldn't be so bad after all, and it helped that it wasn't so hot anymore and that the days were crisp and blue. The disaster with the tomatoes was forgotten; all the rows of dead plants were still out there in the fields, but now there was a sense that things were going to finish well. There would still be some frantic feelings until the frost, but with it there would come a sudden quiet, and everyone could regroup.

*

Sarah and I walked up the hill to join everyone picking the patch on the Hilltop, three long rows of canes that stretched out across the rise, a thousand feet each. It was a beautiful afternoon. The dry dust on the road was as soft as sifted flour, and the rows of raspberries were deep green. The red Chevy was parked halfway down, and we walked there to get empty flats. The metal floor of the truck bed was already full of raspberries, and the picking was just getting started. Eight or ten people were spaced out unevenly in the field, and we found an area that hadn't been covered yet and got started. The berries filled the boxes quickly, and the piles in the truck got taller as the afternoon wore on.

There were bees everywhere as we picked, frantically collecting the sugar from the berries before the frost came. They swarmed on every cane, crawling over the berries, probing and wiggling, and surrounding the flats like a cloud of charged particles. Late in the afternoon there was a sudden shout when one of the apprentices got stung and a dog asleep in the shadow of the truck suddenly jumped up like she'd felt it herself. She bolted across the field barking madly, overcompensating for the fact that she'd been caught off guard.

By mid-afternoon a few clouds had gathered, and it looked like it might rain. Everyone was suddenly in a huge hurry so that the berries wouldn't get wet. We finished the flats we'd been working on and marked our spots in the rows, and then we drove down the hill just as the first fat drops were falling in the dust. The raspberries would make a serious dent in the shortfall that season. More than that though, they restored a sense of optimism and helped make the season feel like it had been worth the hard work. At the end of December the entire crew of apprentices would sign on to come back and work again for the next season.

*

By the last week of September it was officially fall. The ridge had gone orange and red except for veins of dark green where the scrub pines grew, the meadows were gold, and clouds of small birds came up out of the corn stubble, arched into the blue sky, and dove back in. The creek had gone clear, so the fish were visible above the stones, and in the evenings long, ragged Vs of brown geese came over the ridge and down the line of the creek, honking purposefully. Sarah started to wear one of my old Cornell sweatshirts in the mornings, and I wore an insulated flannel shirt. At night the tent was cozy and warm, and we snuggled deeper in our sleeping bags and slept hard.

Before the season ended there was one more thing I wanted to do: finish the shelter the way I'd first imagined it when I'd started building that June. I had the floor already, the platform where we'd been pitching our tent, and I was still in love with it—the way it felt to stand up in the trees, how even and symmetrical it was, how heavy and solid the foundation posts were. Now that it was getting colder we needed a shelter, something with a roof, and what I had in mind was just one room, perfectly square, with space for some bookshelves, two chairs, a small table, and a bed.

I went out to the barnyard and looked at the outbuildings. A small tractor shed, just big enough for one piece of equipment, was the right size and shape, so I spent a few minutes examining it and noting how everything came together. I saw how the walls were braced, how the rafters worked, and how the metal roof connected to them. I didn't bother making any sketches this time, just added up the amounts of lumber I needed and then went back to the lumberyard to buy it, along with some screen for the windows and sheets of tin for the roof. The next morning I put all the tools I needed in a five-gallon bucket—a hammer, saw, measuring tape, and a box of nails—and walked out to get started.

I wasn't in a hurry; it was nice to be building again. A dog had come with me, picking her way down the little winding path that had been worn in the weeds, and she settled in the shade under the floor with a long sigh, stretched her legs once, and went to sleep. I got the corner posts up and connected the tops of them with heavy two by sixes, and I braced the walls diagonally so that they would stand on their own. Over the next three or four days I put up the rafters and the stringers, and eventually I climbed on top and pulled the sheets of tin up and nailed them down.

Once the roof was up I sided the whole building in rough pine slabs, still bright yellow from the mill. I put them up one by one, pressing the next one up against the last, closing in the space as I went. The wood felt tender as it pressed together neatly: the nails sank into the soft planks and gave off a warm smell of sap in the autumn sun. When I was finished, the building felt both flexible and tight, like a woven basket.

The best part of the building had always been how it felt like it was floating up in the trees, and I'd been worried that the addition would mar the effect. If anything, it enhanced it; the walls served to screen the view of the lower elevations and there was no way now, while standing anywhere on the floor, that I could see where the building was anchored or exactly how high I was off the ground. I'd left the front of the shelter mostly open, with screened windows, to maintain the view of the fields and the creek, and from where I stood inside, I could see the front half of the floor, now a kind of porch, stretch out like a long and narrow catwalk above the trees.

The two red canvas camp chairs were still out at the very edge. I sat and smoked a cigarette and looked down over the field, keeping an eye out for deer and groundhogs. The view was different than it had been in the months before; there was winter squash in the field now instead of cabbages. The trailing plants made an even green blanket, and the surrounding foxtails were brittle and yellow. The trees at the edge of the creek were more spare, and I could see the creek glinting.

There was one obvious problem with the building that still had to be resolved: there was no door. There was an informal entrance through the back wall, a gap I'd left between the planks, but eventually I would need to close the building up. I'd thought about a ladder that I could pull up after me, or even just a rope with knots in it, but I was afraid they would both be too much hassle, so I settled on a trapdoor. I could build a set of stairs underneath the platform and cut a hatch through the floor. It would be an elegant solution, and it would make the shelter seem even more like my own little boat in the wilderness.

It felt well built, and part of me wanted it to start raining right then, for the trees to lash in the wind and the rain to pound on the thin metal roof, so I could sit inside and light the lantern, read a book, and have a drink while the water poured off and splashed into the grass.

We wouldn't have much more time to enjoy this building because Sarah would be leaving in two weeks, and I was planning to leave right after Christmas. She was heading to San Francisco, going to look for a job at a museum, and I'd follow her soon after and find a job of my own. I would have two months to live in the building alone, and by the time I left in late December the jar of water I kept under the bed would be frozen solid when I woke up in the morning. The last night I slept there was a little sad but tempered by the knowledge that the roof would hold against the heavy snow, and in the spring the trailing vines would make more progress, and in the summer the blackberry bushes would grow tight against the back wall.

✳

The next harvest of raspberries was even heavier than the one earlier in the week, and my father hadn't had any more luck finding buyers. We'd started freezing the extras, but we needed space to store them. So on a Friday I drove a truck to the ice factory in Huntingdon, a brick warehouse on the edge of town marked by a blue and red sign with white icicles hanging from the bottoms of the letters. The ice business was a fading industry, and there was no one at the receptionist's desk to greet me. I walked down long halls filled with old pieces of equipment, and eventually I found a man in an empty office. He put his magazine down and pulled on a thick jacket with a fur hood.

There was a heavy wooden door behind his desk. He unlocked it and walked through. I followed him in as he flicked on the lights. The freezer was as big as an airplane hangar, a vast space with a soaring ceiling where a frozen mist had collected. There were stacks of bagged ice higher than I thought could possibly be stable, skyscrapers of cubes that stretched off across the concrete floor into the distance. He showed me a free spot in a frozen canyon, and then he left me alone. There wasn't anything to steal, and he seemed eager to get out of the cold.

I rolled a pallet of raspberries off the truck and into the freezer. They were bright red, mounded up on the tops of the boxes, a heap of color in all the blank white. I parked the pallet against the wall, one tiny little treasure hidden in a vast forest of tremendous frozen pillars. Everything gleamed under the bright lights. Before I left I wandered around, marveling. It was arctic, silent, and my steps echoed in all the space. It felt comforting somehow to see the raspberries there, a guarantee that my parents would have something good to sell that winter when all the other vegetables at market were roots.

✶

The raspberry harvests started to get overwhelming; apprentices were leaving other jobs undone, and a few local teenagers had been hired to pick after school. Among the buyers was a big gourmet grocery store on P Street in Washington. They didn't usually buy from farms as small as ours, but these were gorgeous berries, consistently large and firm, and genuinely local. On a Thursday afternoon, after my father had secured a commitment for thirty flats, he called me to his office and asked me to drive to Washington and deliver them. He wouldn't have admitted to being worried about the delivery, but I could tell he was a little tense.

The last flats came out of the field around six thirty, and I filled the back of the car and made a tall stack in the passenger seat. I strapped them in with the seat belts and turned up the air-conditioning to keep them cool. I got in the driver's seat and felt cramped; the space was full with the smell of ripe raspberries, still warm from the afternoon sun. As I drove out the dirt road toward town, one little bee, a stowaway from the field, crawled out of the flats and made lazy circles. I rolled the window down before I turned onto the hard road and he flowed out into the warm air, escaping to the meadows filled with Queen Anne's lace.

I drove the two hours into the city listening to the news on the radio and realized that I hadn't been paying attention to it for months. By the time I came into DC, it was late rush hour, and Massachusetts Avenue was full all the way past the Naval Observatory and down embassy row. Dupont Circle was a crowd of people rushing along the sidewalks, and every one of them seemed to be my age. I could tell they were government workers; the men wore bad ties and the women pastel blouses and black skirts. They collected at the outdoor bars in the warm night, fiddling with the plastic badges on the chains around their necks.

I hadn't been in a big grocery store since I'd left Massachusetts, and I felt out of place in my boots and dirty face, but I reveled in it too. I went in through the front door, past a big display of kiwis, and walked out across the produce section, scuffing my boots a little as I went. A girl picking out zucchini looked at me out of the corner of her eye, and I tipped my hat back and casually tugged on one of my sleeves so that she could see my farmer's tan.

I found the produce manager, a smallish man with a soul patch and a clipboard.

"Are you delivering? You're supposed to go around back, not be out here on the floor."

"Sorry, I've never been here before."

He looked annoyed.

"Well, it's one of the biggest locations in DC. Whatever, what are you delivering?"

"Raspberries."

"How many?"

"Thirty flats."

"Take them around back. Raoul will bring a cart."

He broke off to look at some asparagus and got his walkie-talkie.

"José, get out here and prep this asparagus; it looks like shit. I want an inch off the bottoms of all of these, and get that nasty spinach off the floor too. No, I don't give a shit. Get it off."

He marched away. Feeling slightly giddy and oddly exhilarated, I gave the girl at the zucchini a wink as I walked by again, and she smiled back.

I found the man with the clipboard behind the two metal swinging doors next to the dairy case. He looked at me over his glasses and then at the raspberries. He picked one out and ate it. Then he pointed to a place on the concrete floor.

"Put them over there."

I put them down.

"No. I said there."

He came over and picked through some of the berries on top.

"You from the producer?"

"Yeah, New Morning."

"When did these get picked?"

"This afternoon."

He looked at me and narrowed his eyes, then gave a little smile meant to show that it was cool. We were co-conspirators—I could tell him the truth.

"We picked them three hours ago. I was in the field myself. It's my family's farm."

He looked back at the berries, picked out one that looked fine to me, and threw it in the trash.

"Well, I guess we'll take them. Committed to them now anyway."

He ripped a check out of his book and handed it to me.

"You can go."

I signed his form and turned to go, walking around a pallet of bananas. I got lost behind the dairy cases and took a wrong turn at the cardboard baler. I turned around and was approaching the spot where I'd set down the flats when I heard the produce manager talking to someone else.

"Yo Sam, you see these?"

"Yeah, fucking beautiful."

"These things are going to go fast as hell. We need to put up a display at the front."

There was a long pause. Then the produce manager spoke again in a tone that a basketball fan might use to celebrate an unlikely three-point shot. "Holy FUCKING raspberries!"

I pushed the swinging doors open and went back to where I'd parked the car beside the dumpsters. I drove home in the dark, and when I pulled into the barnyard I could see that the light in my father's office was still on. I knocked on his door and told him that I was home and that everything had gone smoothly. "What did they say about the berries?" I considered telling him the whole story, about how they'd pretended that they weren't any good, but then I decided to skip it. "They loved them. Said they thought they were amazing." My father tipped back in his chair and stared at the black window. "They are amazing. They're lucky to get them."

I understood how my father felt. Delivering those raspberries that afternoon had felt like the inevitable conclusion of a well-executed plan. Out of all the mess of the season, the mud and the anxiety, we created a few perfect things. It seemed like an amazing way to make a living, so simple and graceful, that it was almost hard to believe it was something we did with our hands.

✳

In the late fall, after the frost and the bulk of the harvest was done, my father always changed. He would suddenly have more time for fun, and he would preside over a harvest party with hayrides and apple bobbing, and later there would be a Halloween get-together where my mother would wear the celeriac costume she'd made out of papier-mâché. Every year in November the crew gathered in our house on a Wednesday night for the final potluck of the season, and we had Russian appetizers while my father poured shot after shot of vodka until the apprentices stumbled out to sleep it off in their cold cabins.

Every fall since I could remember, my father and I had

also taken a camping trip together in northern New England. When I was four or five, we would drive a truck to Cabot Creamery to pick up the bulk order of cheese that my parents would sell for the next six months, and we would stop and camp along the way. We put two mattresses in the back of the empty box truck, and sometimes an upholstered chair, setting up a little room that we could park at campgrounds in the White Mountains. We would get up in the freezing mornings to pee out the back door, and then bundle back up before starting a fire for coffee.

For years it was our tradition to climb Mount Washington. We would hike up through the maples and the birches at the lower altitudes and into the stunted pines higher up, and then traverse the last mile above the tree line across the wide shoulder of the mountain, picking our way from cairn to cairn to the summit. We would have lunch at the top, the wind whipping the windsock at the weather station there, and my father's beard would fill with ice. We would take the cog railway back down, and at the gift shop at the bottom we would always buy my mother a set of souvenir salt and pepper shakers.

This fall we took a trip like we always had, this time to Maine to spend a few days on an island off the coast. One motel was open to accommodate a construction crew installing wind turbines during the off-season, but the island was almost empty. We hiked along the coast and had lunch on the smooth, whale-shaped boulders above the sea, then came back through a windswept graveyard where each stone was surrounded by a rusty wrought-iron fence. That evening my father went down to the docks and talked to the lobstermen about how they ran their business, and that night we cooked four lobsters on the hotplate in our chilly motel room.

In those earlier years, my father and I would spend long hours on the highway together, and he would quiz me on geography or the multiplication tables. When I was a little older, I would read out loud, and we once spent hours in a traffic jam on Route 84 while I read "Master and Man" from a book of short stories by Tolstoy. As I got older, I would tell my father about my work and my relationships, and sometimes he talked about his own life: the challenges of working alone for so many years, how the farm had affected his relationships, and how it had defined so many of his choices.

My father and I have never really talked about the details of the farm. I was never very interested to know more about equipment or soil quality, and he never made me feel any pressure to learn. Like any father and son, we'd had difficult times in our relationship, but our conversations had always continued, and we still had them today. My father had strong beliefs, and he transmitted them intensely. I always knew that he had confidence in me and that he was proud of his son. The farm was his livelihood, but his love for me always felt steady and clear.

✳

A few days after delivering the raspberries I went down to finish the shelter by building the trapdoor. I marked out a rectangle on the floor of the porch and cut an open hatch. I went up to the barnyard and cut two long boards and eight shorter lengths for steps. I got two heavy concrete blocks to use as a foundation, and then I drove everything out to the hill in the pickup. I dug a shallow hole to hold the blocks in place, marked out the angles on the lumber with a pencil, and sawed out a pattern.

I banged everything together, and after an hour or two of work I had a simple staircase. Once it was up I stood back and looked at it. Then I put my weight on the bottom step and rested it there, not quite trusting it yet. When I was sure it was steady, I walked up the stairs. It was a strange feeling rising up through the floor like that, but it was nice. It was a steep staircase, almost a ladder, and I felt like I was ascending to the deck of a ship.

I made a door out of the scraps and placed it back over the hatch and worked the hinges a little to see if they were smooth. The whole thing fit tightly back into the floor, and the edges were all flush. I was glad that the boards all still lined up; it made the door seem sort of hidden. It was heavy, and I jumped up and down on it to make sure it would bear my weight. Then I opened it back up and walked down the stairs.

I went out into the barnyard to see if I could find something to use as a handle. I thought about maybe improvising something simple from a smooth tree branch or just attaching a strap of leather bolted at each end. Someone was changing the cultivator tines on the old Model C, and when he unbolted one, I picked it up and felt the weight of it in my hand.

It had a nice even heft, made of half-inch steel and a little less than a foot long, slightly curved with a pleasant, cool feeling in the metal. The blade had a coating of red rust except at the ends, where the dirt had polished it to a dull silver. Back at the shelter I bolted one of the blades to each side, the bottom and the top. The curve of the blade was raised enough that I could slip my hand under the shallow arch it made. When the door was closed, the tine lay on the open deck, a small curved slice of red steel in the middle of an expanse of wood.

That afternoon I built a simple bed out of more scrap wood that had collected during the building project. I started making something small, a size that felt appropriately spartan for a one-room shack, but then I realized that nothing was stopping me from making it luxurious, so I cut out the lengths for a queen size instead. It was much heavier than it needed to be, with legs made out of posts, thick side rails, and slats cut from the pine slabs I'd used to side the building. I put the mattress from the tent on top, and I made the bed with sheets and blankets. Then I pounded a nail into the rafter right above the head of the bed and hung a kerosene lantern from it. When I was done, I put up three long bookshelves along the wall opposite.

That night Sarah and I climbed up the new stairs and went to bed. I lit the lantern and it sputtered until it caught, and the gas burned steady and clean, hissing as it filled the mantles. I pumped the little metal piston that fed it gas, and it grew brighter on each stroke. The light spilled out between the gaps of the siding, and the windows were deep yellow rectangles. The building sat there on its spindly legs, delicate among the bare branches of the walnut trees. We took off our clothes and got into bed naked.

There were four heavy quilts, but the white sheets were

crisp and cold. We opened up a space under the weight of the blankets and warmed it with our bodies. Our faces were still exposed and our breath showed in the frozen air, but we were warm underneath. The lantern hissed and sputtered and made long shadows on the wall, and we talked about what we might do next, idle planning for the future. After a few minutes I reached my bare arm up into the cold and turned down the knob, and the light guttered and then faded slowly as the mantles burned out.

If I hadn't done a single other thing that summer, the fact of this building would have made the entire experience worthwhile. I loved it for the general idea of its simple shelter, and I loved it for the specific pieces, like the way that the cultivator tine sat on the open floor. And I also loved it because it was a part of the farm, proof that I had been there.

✳

At the beginning of November the frost finally came. Sarah had left for San Francisco the day before Halloween, and I was lying on the bed I'd built and thinking about her. It was a warm afternoon for the season, and I watched a bee make loop-de-loops in the air above me, occasionally rising too high on a current of air and bumping against the tin. Eventually it drifted out and floated off through the trees. People were laughing in the field below while they collected winter squash, and I sat on the platform and watched them. I was happy not to be working, and I liked that they couldn't see me in the trees.

They collected the hard, cured winter squash into big piles, some of dark-green acorn, some of tan butternut, and others

of little speckled delicata. They finished the piles, and someone moved the tractor close and lowered a wooden bin on
the front forks. One person stood inside the bin while the
others stood at the piles and tossed the squash across the field
to him. The tossing of the squash was like a game, and the
catcher had to be in constant motion, turning toward the various throwers. The squash came in long gentle arcs, and the
catcher absorbed the weight of them with a swooping movement of his arm.

It was late afternoon and the pale moon was half dissolved.
It wasn't quite full—the harvest moon had been a few weeks
before—but it was large, and I knew that night everything
would freeze in its white light, the stalks of the grass and the
leaves on the trees, the rime of ice clinging to the edge of the
creek. I could hear the leaves in the trees, the dry sound of
early fall, a crow call way off, and under it all the quiet sound
of the creek. For just a brief second I had the feeling of being
glad to be alive at that exact moment. The anxiety of time
receded back to its furthest point, and the present took up all
the available space.

I suddenly wanted to find my mother and father and tell
them that I loved them. I wanted to stay here forever in the
hollow, closed off from the world, in the shelter I'd built, with
a table and a chair, a bed and full bookshelf. I wanted my
grave dug under the black walnut, with Sarah's there beside
it, our children to plant a forsythia that would bloom in the
spring, the first yellow flowers of March. I wanted our bones
to molder and the stone to grow dim, the rain to seep into the

box and the tree roots to grow down through it, and someday the creek to rise and wash us all away.

The folk songs that had been played at Bert's funeral hadn't
just been about sadness and want. For every lament there was
another about the love for a good Kentucky horse or a clear,
cold draw with the first flowers of spring on the grassy banks.
Those were the tunes I wanted to hear in that moment, the
ones with the quick fiddle, the rough washboard, the Jew's harp.
They weren't my songs—I hadn't truly earned them and, if I
was honest, I didn't want to—but I could borrow them for a
minute and take pleasure in what they had to offer. In that cool
air, under that faint moon, I could enjoy being a farmer's son.

A shout came from below as someone got hit in the back
by a badly thrown squash, and the spell was broken. I could
already feel the nostalgia for that moment, now lost, what
had seemed like an experience of grace. I wanted this land to
always be ours, but I knew that the farm couldn't last forever.
I knew that there wouldn't always be another summer here
for me, that my mother and father wouldn't always be waiting
in this hollow when I needed to go home and hide. No matter
how hard my father worked or how much he worried, the
farm couldn't save us in the very end.

Now the people in the field were finishing up, and they
gathered around the tractor to go back up to the barnyard. I
stood up and called down to them, and they all turned at
once, surprised to see that I'd been spying. Someone shouted,
"Hey, Arlo!" and I waved and yelled that they should wait for
me. I made my way down the grassy slope, picking my way

through the briars and the cattails that separated the hill from the field. I climbed up on the wagon with the rest of them. The smell of tractor exhaust was sharp in the cold air, and there was a heavy jerk as it slid into gear and started moving. I stood next to the bin of squash, resting my hand on the curve of a butternut, warm from where it had sat in the sun. I looked out across the field, surveying my domain, and then it was gone behind the border of trees.

*

After Christmas I left the farm to join Sarah and eventually found a job in San Francisco in a natural foods store that specialized in produce. I started work early when it was still dark and spent the mornings stacking clementines, lettuce, and celery. It was nice working with vegetables, and much easier than actually working in the fields, and it kept me busy and paid the rent. I still hadn't solved the problem of what I wanted to do with my life—the same problem that I had in Massachusetts was still with me now. I was coming to the realization that it would probably be with me forever, and that it was a problem that I likely shared with every other person on earth.

I wasn't completely at sea in San Francisco though. I'd always loved to read—the lack of a television on the farm would have forced me to it anyway—and now I started to write. Sarah found an old desk on the street and painted it blue, and in the evenings I sat there and worked. Like my mother and father's first season at New Morning, the results came hard, but I enjoyed it, and occasionally it felt like I was doing something useful.

After the next Thanksgiving, Sarah and I went back to the farm together for a week to visit with my parents. The light was pale, and the trees were all dark and bare as we drove down the dirt road; the tops of the ridges were pink in the last light. My sister was home, and we all sat at the enameled table in the kitchen for an hour or two, drank beer, argued with each other, and played a game of Scrabble. Before it got dark Sarah and I walked out behind the barn to the shelter. The wood was a little weathered and gray, but the foundation was solid and the roof was sound. Hornets had built a paper nest in one of the corners, and there were perfect cones of sawdust on the bed left by carpenter bees.

There was a rustle behind the few books left on the shelves, and I paused. A house sparrow had built her nest in the space, and she scolded me loudly and beat her wings, trying desperately to scare me off. She flew to perch on the top of one of the windows, cocked her head, and watched me. I looked at her little nest, lined with feathers and soft bits of hay and grass, cozy looking and well built. I left the books behind and closed the trapdoor over my head. I found Sarah lying in the tall grass of the meadow above, offered her my hand and pulled her up, and we went back toward the house.

We walked across the fields in the last light. The farm was mostly quiet in these short days, the rye grass seeded on the fallow fields, and the ground was frozen, too hard to do any useful work. If there was a still point in the seasons, a moment when things ended, it was now. The fields were empty of everything but a few dried stalks, the scenery lonely and demanding quiet, like a graveyard. Someday, many years on, I hope, I will come back here to see this land as a memorial to my parents. The sumac and the volunteer saplings will have grown up at the edges of the fields, and some of them will be gone altogether, just faint depressions in the grass.

There was still life here now though. The mice were huddled in the dark corners of the barn, the wasps in the eaves, and that sparrow slept in her nest behind the books. My mother had strung a line of Christmas lights around the front door, and a dog sat in their glow, his tail thumping up little clouds of dust from the concrete porch. Through the window I could see everyone I loved sitting around the table. Soon we'd leave these acres again, back to other houses, towns, and cities, out to all the other places we were from. But here, on the farm, we were all together, my family held in this hollow of the land.

ACKNOWLEDGMENTS

I would like to thank my agent, Chris Parris-Lamb, for his bracing enthusiasm and razor-sharp taste, my editor, Sarah Bowlin, for her tireless attention to fine detail and her unerring ability to see the bigger picture, Katie Kurtzman for her determined advocacy, Andy Kifer and Joanna Levine for all their kind help, and everyone else at the Gernert Company and Henry Holt.

Deep appreciation to Philip Post, Joel Chace, and Suzanne Wootton for the decades they've given to introducing students to the great writers, and Christina Thompson for giving me the confidence to finally write something of my own.

My loving gratitude to my mother for her many thoughtful readings of the manuscript, even when there were beans to pack, to my father for never once questioning whether or not this was a good plan, and to my sister, Janie, for always making me feel that she's proud of her big brother.

The writing of this book would not have been possible without the selfless support, patience, encouragement and trust of my wife, Sarah. I love you.